the

extraordinariness

of the

christian

life

A Bible Study on the Sermon on the Mount

by Dietrich Bonhoeffer

NATIONAL STUDENT CHRISTIAN FEDERATION
NEW YORK, NEW YORK

Price: Single copy $1.00

NATIONAL STUDENT CHRISTIAN FEDERATION
475 Riverside Drive, New York, N.Y.   10027

PRINTED IN THE USA

Book design and printing by
SOWERS PRINTING COMPANY, LEBANON, PA.

 2

Contents

Contents

Introduction

THIS introduction might actually be understood better if it were read as an epilogue. For it is addressed to a question which may not now be on your mind, but which will arise for many as they take up Bonhoeffer's study of the Sermon on the Mount. And this is the question: Is there any continuity between the study of the mission of the church suggested to us through Alexander Schmemann's book *For The Life Of The World,* and the study of the Sermon on the Mount under the guidance of Dietrich Bonhoeffer's comments? Or are we, after having made a sacramental emphasis for a little while, back on our old familiar Protestant stumping grounds?

Bonhoeffer and Schmemann may appear to be complete strangers to each other. But it is one of the exciting aspects of the ecumenical movement that in ecumenical fellowship we discover one another. Furthermore, the decisive issues concerning the Christian faith are drawing new lines today, bringing together apparent strangers and revealing distance between neighbors. Latter-day 'Honest-to-God' theology would have us believe that Bonhoeffer belongs among the theological existentialists, together with Bultmann and Tillich. A reading of this Bible study in the light of, or rather surrounded by, the *leitourgia* of the Church in the Orthodox sense, might clear up some of the confusion and reveal a more authentic bond of ecumenical fellowship.

We are *not* talking about like-mindedness, an un-Christian category that today is no less than segregationist. We are talking about a bond of ecumenical fellowship. Within this fellowship real conversation will be possible which will also include the frank exploration of the differences. For there *are* differences between these two books and their authors, but they will matter only when we see that the authors are standing on a common ground and thinking within a common framework. In the following remarks a few pointers are provided which may lead to the discovery of this common ground and of the meaningful differences. The intention is to give encouragement to the readers of the Bible study to go beyond these brief pointers.

"Not of this world . . ." While reading Schmemann's *For The Life Of The World* I sometimes felt that it was almost "too good to be true," too "heavenly." The Protestant in me, while admiring and even envying the richness of liturgical life, kept

1

asking what this all had to do with the 20th century world of automation, of the race revolution and the space revolution. How is it relevant, what help is it to us in meeting today's problems? And it seemed infuriating to the ineradicably utilitarian Protestant mind to hear Schmemann's categorical answer that "The purpose of Christianity is not to help people . . . but to reveal the Truth about life and death in order that people may be saved by this Truth." (p. 74) This Truth is made plain, Schmemann maintains, in the liturgy, the sacraments of Eurcharist, matrimony and ordination. In all this the Church testifies to the fact "that in the world in which Christ died, 'natural life' has been brought to its end." (p. 12)

The Church's life, then, is not of this world, it is esoteric in relation to this world; it is life of and in the Kingdom, the joy of the Eucharist. Why this stress on its esoteric character? If we have been tempted to charge it to an Eastern mystical or sacramental tradition we will now find that we have also Bonhoeffer against us. All we need is to remind ourselves of the Beatitudes which Bonhoeffer interprets to us with such poignancy and force. For *who* is blessed? Bonhoeffer answers: the disciples, those who are called by Jesus and who, therefore, "stand as strangers in the world in the power of him who was such a stranger to the world that it crucified him. The blessing is upon those who "Show by every word and deed that they do not belong to this earth." (p. 10, 11)

". . . but for the sake of this world." It would seem that, given the esoteric character of the Church's life, the Church and the world could each go its own merry or not so merry way. But "not of this world" does not mean "apart from the world," either for Bonhoeffer or for Schmemann. As Bonhoeffer shows in the first part of *The Cost of Discipleship,* this logic was adopted during some periods of the Church's history, notably in the monastic movement. It is the world's logic and Luther's return from the cloister was, therefore, "The worst blow the world had suffered since the days of early Christianity." The Church, called out by God from among the people, is now set in the midst of the world. This is why Bonhoeffer is careful in describing the scene of the Sermon on the Mount: "Jesus calls his disciples blessed in the hearing of the crowd, and the crowd is called upon as a startled witness." Christian life is in the midst of life *on behalf* of the world. In this connection Schmemann emphasizes the *priestly* character of the new life. "Man was created priest of the world, the one who offers the world to God in a sacrifice of love and praise." The vocation of the ordained priest is "to reveal to each vocation its priestly essence, to make the whole life of all men the liturgy of the Kingdom, to reveal the Church as the Royal Priesthood of the redeemed world." (69) And Bonhoeffer: "If we pray for them, we are taking their distress and poverty, their guilt and perdition upon ourselves, and pleading to God for them. We are doing vicariously for them what they cannot do for themselves." (54) This is the meaning of love of the enemy!

It may be worthwhile to dwell a moment on this point of the vicarious or priestly existence of the Christian. For what is at stake here seems to me absolutely fundamental for our Christian existence in the 20th century America. To use a different idiom, it concerns the truly *public* character of the Christian life. *Life for the world is life in full view of the world.* The life and joy of the Kingdom (Schmemann) or the life of discipleship (Bonhoeffer) is not a life behind closed doors, but in the streets amidst "the down-trodden, the sick, the wretched, the wronged the outcast." (Bon. p. 12) Where this word is heard it will hit like a bomb and explode the fallacy of our privatized modern Christianity. For it seems that whatever little faith, joy, or hope we muster, we keep it bottled up within ourselves, afraid to let anyone glimpse it. Who among us knows what it really means to *share* life, our worries, sorrows, joys? Our gatherings in the churches and in campus Christian groups more often than not turn into sessions of "making it" in group life without ever leading to real participation in the groups. I am afraid that unless we are willing to be pulled out of this make-believe existence into the community of believers we will not understand either Schmemann or Bonhoeffer. Life in the Kingdom, the life of discipleship is the end of the world's life, the end of private life; but it is the beginning of the life *for the sake* of the world.

"For the Life of the World." The title of Father Schmemann's book, then, expresses the common ground on which both authors stand. This does not mean that their focus is necessarily the same. Obviously there are differences. We meet two men who stand in different strands of the Church's tradition, one shaped in the Eastern, the other in the Western world. But these are not always fruitful distinctions. They tend to force us to take sides. We must learn to look at differences not for the purpose of taking sides, but in order to penetrate deeper into the understandings of both sides. Let me suggest one distinction which might be helpful in this regard.

It might be said that Father Schmemann succeeds best, where he shows that the Church in submission to, and conformity with its Lord, exists "For the *Life* of the World." It exhibits this new life of the world to come. Its existence, particularly its liturgy, is nothing but a series of variations on the theme of this new life. Perhaps the most "extreme" way of stating this emphasis is contained in the affirmation that "through the cross joy came to the whole world. . . ."

Joy—through the cross. This sounds as "un-Protestant" as anything. In the Protestant book it would read rather: judgement through the cross. Indeed, what Bonhoeffer says about the cross relates rather to the judgement than to joy. Bonhoeffer's concern might be pointed out by underlining the last word of the title: "For the Life of the *World*."

Surely Bonhoeffer, too, knows the new life; he knows that discipleship is first of all a *blessed* state. But now this is to be lived in *this world*. And it is *this world* which confronts Bonhoeffer with all its dynamic and demonic expressions. He knows that when the joy of the new life becomes manifest in this world, it will be exposed to hostility, ridicule, persecution. The world will want to get rid of it. Schmemann, too, knows this world, and yet he does not seem to be concerned about its opposition. This is not optimism. Rather, it seems to me that in the Orthodox Liturgy there is something of that heavenly laughter of Psalm 2.

We may first have to learn Bonhoeffer's knowledge of this world before we can participate in the "laughter" with the angels. For, caught as we are, in an optimism which is about to revert into a pessimism or nihilism, it is well to learn from a man who witnessed the breakdown of the religious and cultural foundations in his life. Bonhoeffer wrote this study in the 1930's during the Hitler regime. His eyes and senses were sharpened as a result of the trial which he and his church underwent. Such are God's gifts in times of trial. Thus his pen is sharp, too. Through his words the Sermon on the Mount cuts to the bone. It is rare that a Bible study after almost 30 years still speaks with such freshness and directness across the changing times and generations. For we are a different generation, but Dietrich Bonhoeffer may reach us across this barrier because he, like Alexander Schmemann, is reaching down to the fundamentals of life.

New York   THOMAS WIESER
November 22, 1963

1

The Beatitudes

Matt. 5.1-12

LET US picture the scene: Jesus on the mountain, the multitudes, and the disciples. The *people* see Jesus with his disciples, who have gathered around him. Until quite recently these men had been completely identified with the multitude, they were just like the rest. Then came the call of Jesus, and at once they left all and followed him. Since then they have belonged to him, body and soul. Now they go with him, live with him, and follow him wherever he leads them. Something unique had occurred to them. That disconcerting and offensive fact stares the people in the face. The *disciples* see the people, from whose midst they themselves have come. These people are the lost sheep of the house of Israel, the elect people of God, the "national Church." When the call of Jesus had selected them from among the people, the disciples had done what for the lost sheep of the house of Israel was the only natural and necessary thing to do—they had followed the voice of the Good Shepherd, because they knew his voice. Thus their very action in enlisting as disciples proves that they

5

are members of this people; they will live among
them, going into their midst, and preaching the call
of Jesus and the glory of discipleship. But what will
the end be? *Jesus* sees his disciples. They have publicly left the crowd to join him. He has called them,
every one, and they have renounced everything at
his call. Now they are living in want and privation,
the poorest of the poor, the sorest afflicted, and the
hungriest of the hungry. They have only him, and
with him they have nothing, literally nothing in the
world, but everything with and through God. It is
but a little flock he has found, and it is a great flock
he is seeking as he looks at the people. Disciples and
people, they belong together. The disciples will be his
messengers and here and there they will find men to
hear and believe their message. Yet there will be
enmity between them right to the bitter end. All the
wrath of God's people against him and his Word will
fall on his disciples; his rejection will be theirs. The
cross casts its shadow before. Christ, the disciples, and
the people—the stage is already set for the passion of
Jesus and his Church.[1]

Therefore Jesus calls his disciples blessed (cf. Luke
6.20 ff). He spoke to men who had already responded
to the power of his call, and it is that call which has
made them poor, afflicted and hungry. He calls them
blessed, not because of their privation, or the renunciation they have made, for these are not blessed in
themselves. Only the call and the promise, for the
sake of which they are ready to suffer poverty and
renunciation, can justify the beatitudes. Admittedly,

[1] The warrant for this exposition lies in the phrase ἀνοίξας
τὸ στόμα. Even in the early Church this point was emphasized.
Before Jesus speaks there is a pause—all is silent for a moment
or two.

Jesus sometimes speaks of privation and sometimes of deliberate renunciation as if they implied particular virtues in his disciples, but that is neither here nor there. External privation and personal renunciation both have the same ground—the call and the promise of Jesus. Neither possesses any intrinsic claim to recognition.[1]

Jesus calls his disciples blessed in the hearing of the crowd, and the crowd is called upon as a startled witness. The heritage which God had promised to Israel as a whole is here attributed to the little flock of disciples whom Jesus had chosen. "Theirs is the kingdom of heaven." But disciples and people are one, for they are all members of the Church which is called of God. Hence the aim of this beatitude is to bring *all* who hear it to decision and salvation. All are called to be what in the reality of God they are already. The disciples are called blessed because they have obeyed the call of Jesus, and the people as a whole because they are heirs of the promise. But will

---

[1] There is no justification whatever for setting Luke's version of the beatitudes over against Matthew's. Matthew is not spiritualizing the beatitudes, and Luke giving them in their original form, nor is Luke giving a political twist to an original form of the beatitude which applied only to a poverty of disposition. Privation is not the ground of the beatitude in Luke, nor renunciation in Matthew. On the contrary, both gospels recognize that neither privation nor renunciation, spiritual or political, is justified, except by the call and promise of Jesus, who alone makes blessed those whom he calls, and who is in his person the sole ground of their beatitude. Since the days of the Clementines, Catholic exegesis has applied this beatitude to the virtue of poverty, the *paupertas voluntaria* of the monks, or any kind of poverty undertaken voluntarily for the sake of Christ. But in both cases the error lies in looking for some kind of human behaviour as the ground for the beatitude instead of the call and promise of Jesus alone.

they now claim their heritage by believing in Jesus Christ and his word? Or will they fall into apostasy by refusing to accept him? That is the question which still remains to be answered.

"Blessed are the poor in spirit, for theirs is the kingdom of heaven." Privation is the lot of the disciples in every sphere of their lives. They are the "poor" *tout court* (Luke 6.20). They have no security, no possessions to call their own, not even a foot of earth to call their home, no earthly society to claim their absolute allegiance. Nay more, they have no spiritual power, experience or knowledge to afford them consolation or security. For his sake they have lost all. In following him they lost even their own selves, and everything that could make them rich. Now they are poor—so inexperienced, so stupid, that they have no other hope but him who called them. Jesus knows all about the others too, the representatives and preachers of the national religion, who enjoy greatness and renown, whose feet are firmly planted on the earth, who are deeply rooted in the culture and piety of the people and moulded by the spirit of the age. Yet it is not they, but the disciples who are called blessed—*theirs* is the kingdom of heaven. That kingdom dawns on *them*, the little band who for the sake of Jesus live a life of absolute renunciation and poverty. And in that very poverty they are heirs of the kingdom. They have their treasure in secret, they find it on the cross. And they have the promise that they will one day visibly enjoy the glory of the kingdom, which in principle is already realized in the utter poverty of the cross.

This beatitude is poles removed from the caricatures of it which appear in political and social manifestos. The Antichrist also calls the poor blessed, but not for

the sake of the cross, which embraces all poverty and
transforms it into a source of blessing. He fights the
cross with political and sociological ideology. He may
call it Christian, but that only makes him a still more
dangerous enemy.

*"Blessed are they that mourn, for they shalll be
comforted."* With each beatitude the gulf is widened
between the disciples and the people, their call to
come forth from the people becomes increasingly
manifest. By "mourning" Jesus, of course, means
doing without what the world calls peace and pros-
perity: He means refusing to be in tune with the
world or to accommodate oneself to its standards.
Such men mourn for the world, for its guilt, its fate
and its fortune. While the world keeps holiday they
stand aside, and while the world sings, "Gather ye
rose-buds while ye may," they mourn. They see that
for all the jollity on board, the ship is beginning
to sink. The world dreams of progress, of power and
of the future, but the disciples meditate on the end,
the last judgement, and the coming of the kingdom.
To such heights the world cannot rise. And so the disciples are strangers in the world, unwelcome guests
and disturbers of the peace. No wonder the world
rejects them! Why does the Christian Church so
often have to look on from outside when the nation
is celebrating? Have churchmen no understanding
and sympathy for their fellow-men? Have they
become victims of misanthropy? Nobody loves his
fellow-men better than a disciple, nobody understands his fellow-men better. than the Christian
fellowship, and that very love impels them to stand
aside and mourn. It was a happy and suggestive
thought of Luther, to translate the Greek word here
by the German *Leidtragen* (sorrow-bearing). For the

emphasis lies on the *bearing* of sorrow. The disciple-community does not shake off sorrow as though it were no concern of its own, but willingly bears it. And in this way they show how close are the bonds which bind them to the rest of humanity. But at the same time they do not go out of their way to look for suffering, or try to contract out of it by adopting an attitude of contempt and disdain. They simply bear the suffering which comes their way as they try to follow Jesus Christ, and bear it for *his* sake. Sorrow cannot tire them or wear them down, it cannot embitter them or cause them to break down under the strain; far from it, for they bear their sorrow in the strength of him who bears them up, who bore the whole suffering of the world upon the cross. They stand as the bearers of sorrow in the fellowship of the Crucified: they stand as strangers in the world in the power of him who was such a stranger to the world that it crucified him. This is their comfort, or better still, this *Man* is their comfort, the Comforter (cf. Luke 2.25). The community of strangers find their comfort in the cross, they are comforted by being cast upon the place where the Comforter of Israel awaits them. Thus do they find their true home with their crucified Lord, both here and in eternity.

"Blessed are the meek: for they shall inherit the earth." This community of strangers possesses no inherent right of its own to protect its members in the world, nor do they claim such rights, for they are meek, they renounce every right of their own and live for the sake of Jesus Christ. When reproached, they hold their peace; when treated with violence they endure it patiently; when men drive them from their presence, they yield their ground. They will not go to law to defend their rights, or make a scene when they

suffer injustice, nor do they insist on their legal rights. They are determined to leave their rights to God alone—*non cupidi vindictae,* as the ancient Church paraphrased it. Their right is in the will of their Lord —that and no more. They show by every word and gesture that they do not belong to this earth. Leave heaven to them, says the world in its pity, that is where they belong.[1] But Jesus says: "They shall inherit the earth." To these, the powerless and the disenfranchised, the very earth belongs. Those who now possess it by violence and injustice shall lose it, and those who here have utterly renounced it, who were meek to the point of the cross, shall rule the new earth. We must not interpret this as a reference to God's exercise of juridicial punishment within the world, as Calvin did: what it means is that when the kingdom of heaven descends, the face of the earth will be renewed, and it will belong to the flock of Jesus. God does not forsake the earth: he made it, he sent his Son to it, and on it he built his Church. Thus a beginning has already been made in this present age. A sign has been given. The powerless have here and now received a plot of earth, for they have the Church and its fellowship, its goods, its brothers and sisters, in the midst of persecutions even to the length of the cross. The renewal of the earth begins at Golgotha, where the meek One died, and from thence it will spread. When the kingdom finally comes, the meek shall possess the earth.

"Blessed are they that hunger and thirst after righteousness: for they shall be filled." Not only do the followers of Jesus renounce their rights, they

---

[1] The Emperor Julian wrote mockingly in a letter (No. 43) that he only confiscated the property of Christians so as to make them poor enough to enter the kingdom of heaven.

renounce their own righteousness too. They get no praise for their achievements or sacrifices. They cannot have righteousness except by hungering and thirsting for it (this applies equally to their own righteousness and to the righteousness of God on earth), always they look forward to the future righteousness of God, but they cannot establish it for themselves. Those who follow Jesus grow hungry and thirsty on the way. They are longing for the forgiveness of all sin, for complete renewal, for the renewal too of the earth and the full establishment of God's law. They are still involved in the world's curse, and affected by its sin. He whom they follow must die accursed on the cross, with a desperate cry for righteousness on his lips: "My God, my God, why hast thou forsaken me?" But the disciple is not above his master, he follows in his steps. Happy are they who have the promise that they shall be filled, for the righteousness they receive will be no empty promise, but real satisfaction. They will eat the Bread of Life in the Messianic Feast. They are blessed because they already enjoy this bread here and now, for in their hunger they are sustained by the bread of life, the bliss of sinners.

"Blessed are the merciful, for they shall obtain mercy." These men without possessions or power, these strangers on earth, these sinners, these followers of Jesus, have in their life with him *renounced their own dignity,* for they are merciful. As if their own needs and their own distress were not enough, they take upon themselves the distress and humiliation and sin of others. They have an irresistible love for the down-trodden, the sick, the wretched, the wronged, the outcast and all who are tortured with anxiety. They go out and seek all who are enmeshed in the toils of sin and guilt. No distress is too great, no sin

too appalling for their pity. If any man falls into disgrace, the merciful will sacrifice their own honour to shield him, and take his shame upon themselves. They will be found consorting with publicans and sinners, careless of the shame they incur thereby. In order that they may be merciful they cast away the most priceless treasure of human life, their personal dignity and honour. For the only honour and dignity they know is their Lord's own mercy, to which alone they owe their very lives. He was not ashamed of his disciples, he became the brother of mankind, and bore their shame unto the death of the cross. That is how Jesus, the crucified, was merciful. His followers owe their lives entirely to that mercy. It makes them forget their own honour and dignity, and seek the society of sinners. They are glad to incur reproach, for they know that then they are blessed. One day God himself will come down and take upon himself their sin and shame. He will cover them with his own honour and remove their disgrace. It will be his glory to bear the shame of sinners and to clothe them with his honour. Blessed are the merciful, for they have the Merciful for their Lord.

"*Blessed are the pure in heart: for they shall see God.*" Who is pure in heart? Only those who have surrendered their hearts completely to Jesus that he may reign in them alone. Only those whose hearts are undefiled by their own evil—and by their own virtues too. The pure in heart have a child-like simplicity like Adam before the fall, innocent alike of good and evil: their hearts are not ruled by their conscience, but by the will of Jesus. If men renounce their own good, if in penitence they have renounced their own hearts, if they rely solely upon Jesus, then his word purifies their hearts. Purity of heart is here contrasted with all outward purity, even the purity of high intentions. The pure heart is pure alike of good and evil, it belongs exclusively to Christ and looks only to him who goes on before. Only they will see God, who in this life have looked solely unto Jesus Christ, the Son of God. For then their hearts are free from all defiling phantasies and are not distracted by conflicting desires and intentions. They are wholly absorbed by the contemplation of God. They shall see God, whose hearts have become a reflection of the image of Jesus Christ.

"Blessed are the peacemakers: for they shall be called the children of God." The followers of Jesus have been called to peace. When he called them they found their peace, for he is their peace. But now they are told that they must not only *have* peace but *make* it.[1] And to that end they renounce all violence and tumult. In the cause of Christ nothing is to be gained by such methods. His kingdom is one of peace, and the mutual greeting of his flock is a greeting of peace. His disciples keep the peace by choosing to endure suffering themselves rather than inflict it on others. They maintain fellowship where others would break it off. They renounce all self-assertion, and quietly suffer in the face of hatred and wrong. In so doing they overcome evil with good, and establish the peace of God in the midst of a world of war and hate. But nowhere will that peace be more manifest than where they meet the wicked in peace and are ready to suffer at their hands. The peacemakers will carry the

---

[1] There is a *double entendre* in the Greek εἰρηνοποιοί. Even Luther's *Friedfertig*, as he himself explained, is not to be taken exclusively in a passive sense. The English translation "peacemakers" is one-sided, and has encouraged a Pelagian and activistic interpretation of this beatitude.

cross with their Lord, for it was on the cross that
peace was made. Now that they are partners in
Christ's work of reconciliation, they are called the
sons of God as he is the Son of God.

"*Blessed are they that have been persecuted for
righteousness' sake: for theirs is the kingdom of
heaven.*" This does not refer to the righteousness of
God, but to suffering in a just cause,[1] suffering for
their own just judgements and actions. For it is by
these that they who renounce possessions, fortune,
rights, righteousness, honour, and force for the sake
of following Christ, will be distinguished from the
world. The world will be offended at them, and so
the disciples will be persecuted for righteousness' sake.
Not recognition, but rejection, is the reward they get
from the world for their message and works. It is
important that Jesus gives his blessing not merely to
suffering incurred directly for the confession of his
name, but to suffering in any just cause. They receive
the same promise as the poor, for in persecution they
are their equals in poverty.

Having reached the end of the beatitudes, we naturally ask if there is any place on this earth for the
community which they describe. Clearly, there is
one place, and only one, and that is where the poorest, meekest, and most sorely tried of all men is to
be found—on the cross at Golgotha. The fellowship
of the beatitudes is the fellowship of the Crucified.
With him it has lost all, and with him it has found
all. From the cross there comes the call "blessed,
blessed." The last beatitude is addressed directly to
the disciples, for only they can understand it, "Blessed
are *ye* when men shall reproach you, and persecute

---

[1] Note the absence of the definite article.

you, and say all manner of evil against you falsely for my sake. Rejoice and be exceeding glad, for great is your reward in heaven: for so persecuted they the prophets which were before you." "For my sake" the disciples are reproached, but because it is for his sake, the reproach falls on him. It is he who bears the guilt. The curse, the deadly persecution and evil slander confirm the blessed state of the disciples in their fellowship with Jesus. It could not be otherwise, for these meek strangers are bound to provoke the world to insult, violence and slander. Too menacing, too loud are the voices of these poor meek men, too patient and too silent their suffering. Too powerful are the testimony of their poverty and their endurance of the wrongs of the world. This is fatal, and so, while Jesus calls them blessed, the world cries: "Away with them, away with them!" Yes, but whither? To the kingdom of heaven. "Rejoice and be exceeding glad: for great is your reward in heaven." There shall the poor be seen in the halls of joy. With his own hand God wipes away the tears from the eyes of those who had mourned upon earth. He feeds the hungry at his Banquet. There stand the scarred bodies of the martyrs, now glorified and clothed in the white robes of eternal righteousness instead of the rags of sin and repentance. The echoes of this joy reach the little flock below as it stands beneath the cross, and they hear Jesus saying: "Blessed are ye!"

2

The Visible Community

Ye are the salt of the earth: but if the salt have lost its savour, wherewith shall it be salted? it is thenceforth good for nothing, but to be cast out and trodden under foot of men. Ye are the light of the world. A city set on a hill cannot be hid. Neither do men light a lamp, and put it under the bushel, but on the stand; and it shineth unto all that are in the house. Even so let your light shine before men, that they may see your good works, and glorify your Father which is in heaven. (Matt. 5.13-16)

THESE WORDS are addressed to the same audience as the beatitudes—to those who are summoned to follow the Crucified in the life of grace. Up to now we must have had the impression that the blessed ones were too good for this world, and only fit to live in heaven. But now Jesus calls them the salt of the earth—salt, the most indispensable necessity of life. The disciples, that is to say, are the highest good, the supreme value which the earth possesses, for without them it cannot live. They are the salt that sustains the earth, for their sake the world exists, yes, for the sake of these, the poor, ignoble and weak, whom the world rejects. In casting out the disciples the earth is destroying its very life. And yet, wonder of wonders, it is for the sake of the outcasts that the earth is allowed to continue. The "divine salt," as Homer called it, maintains itself by fulfilling its proper function. It penetrates the whole earth, and by it the earth subsists. The disciples, then, must not only think of heaven; they have an earthly task as well. Now that they are bound exclusively to Jesus they are told to look at the earth whose salt they are. It is to be noted that Jesus calls not himself, but his disciples the salt of the earth, for he entrusts his work on earth to them. His own work rests with the people of Israel, but the whole earth is committed to the disciples. But only as long as it remains salt and retains its cleansing and savouring properties can the salt preserve the earth. For its own sake, as well as for the sake of the earth, the salt must remain salt, the disciple community must be faithful to the mission which the call of Christ has given it. That will be its proper function on earth and will give it its preservative power. Salt is said to be imperishable; it can never lose its cleansing properties. That is why salt was required in the ritual of the Old Testament sacrifices, and why in the baptismal rite of the Roman Church salt is placed in the infant's mouth (see Ex. 30.35; Ezek. 16.4). In the imperishability of salt we have a guarantee of the permanence of the divine community.

"Ye are the salt." Jesus does not say: "You *must* be the salt." It is not for the disciples to decide whether they will be the salt of the earth, for they are so whether they like it or not, they have been made salt by the call they have received. Again, it is: "Ye *are* the salt," not "Ye *have* the salt." By identifying the salt with the apostolic proclamation the Reformers robbed the saying of all its sting. No, the word speaks of their whole existence in so far as it is grounded anew in the call of Christ, that same existence which was the burden of the beatitudes. The call of Christ makes those who respond to it the salt of the earth in their total existence.

Of course there is another possibility—the salt may lose its savour and cease to be salt at all. It just stops working. Then it is indeed good for nothing but to be thrown away. That is the peculiar quality of salt. Everything else needs to be seasoned with salt, but once the salt itself has lost its savour, it can never be salted again. Everything else can be saved by salt, however bad it has gone—only salt which loses its savour has no hope of recovery. That is the other side of the picture. That is the judgement which always hangs over the disciple community, whose mission is to save the world, but which, if it ceases to live up to that mission, is itself irretrievably lost. The call of Jesus Christ means either that we are the salt of the earth, or else we are annihilated; either we follow the call or we are crushed beneath it. There is no question of a second chance.

The call of Jesus makes the disciple community not only the salt but also the light of the world: their activity is visible, as well as imperceptible. "Ye *are* the light." Once again it is not: "You are to be the light," they are already the light because Christ has called them, they are a light which is seen of men, they cannot be otherwise, and if they were it would be a sign that they had not been called. How impossible, how utterly absurd it would be for the disciples—*these* disciples, such men as these!—to try and *become* the light of the world! No, they are already the light, and the call has made them so. Nor does Jesus say: "You *have* the light." The light is not an instrument which has been put into their hands, such as their preaching. It is the disciples themselves. The same Jesus who, speaking of himself, said, "I am the light," says to his followers: "You are the light in your whole existence, provided you remain faithful to your calling. And since you are that light, you can no longer remain hidden, even if you want to." It is the property of light to shine. A city set on a hill cannot be hid; it can be seen for miles away, whether it is a fortified burgh, a stronghold or a tottering ruin. This city set on the hill (the Israelite would instinctively think of "Jerusalem on high") is the disciple community. But this is not to say that the disciples have now to make their first decision. The only necessary decision has already been taken. Now they must be what they really are—otherwise they are not followers of Jesus. The followers are a visible community; their discipleship visible in action which lifts them out of the world—otherwise it would not be discipleship. And of course the following is as visible to the world as a light in the darkness or a mountain rising from a plain.

Flight into the invisible is a denial of the call. A community of Jesus which seeks to hide itself has ceased to follow him. "Neither do men light a lamp and put it under a bushel, but on the stand." Once again we are confronted with an alternative; the light may be covered of its own choice; it may be extinguished under a bushel, and the call may be denied. The bushel may be the fear of men, or perhaps deliberate conformity to the world for some ulterior motive, a missionary purpose for example, or a sentimental humanitarianism. But the motive may be more sinister than that; it may be "Reformation theology" which boldly claims the name of *theologia crucis*, and pretends to prefer to Pharisaic ostentation a modest invisibility, which in practice means conformity to the world. When that happens, the hall-mark of the

Church becomes *justitia civilis* instead of extraordinary visibility. The very failure of the light to shine becomes the touchstone of our Christianity. But Jesus says: "Let your light so shine before men." For when all is said and done, it is the light of the call of Jesus Christ which shines here. But what manner of light is it which these followers of Jesus, these disciples of the beatitudes, are to kindle on earth? What sort of light is to shine from the place where only the disciples have a right to be? How are we to reconcile the obscurity of the cross of Christ with the light that shines? Ought not the Christian life to be as obscure as the cross itself? Is not the light exactly what they ought to avoid? It is a wicked sophistry to justify the worldliness of the Church by the cross of Jesus. Is it not plain to the simplest hearer that the cross is the very place where something extraordinary has been made visible? Or is the cross no more than an example of *justitia civilis?* Does it stand for nothing more than worldliness? Did not the cross become extraordinarily visible amongst all the darkness to the terrified spectators? Are the rejection and the suffering of Christ, his death before the gates of the city on the hill of shame, not visible enough? Are they what is meant by "invisibility"?

It is in *this* light that the good works of the disciples are meant to be seen. Men are not to see the disciples but their good works, says Jesus. And these works are none other than those which the Lord Jesus himself has created in them by calling them to be the light of the world under the shadow of his cross. The good works are poverty, peregrination, meekness, peaceableness, and finally persecution and rejection. All these good works are a bearing of the cross of Jesus Christ. The cross is the strange light which alone illuminates these good works of the disciples. Jesus does not say that men will see God; they will see the good works and glorify God for them. The cross and the works of the cross, the poverty and renunciation of the blessed in the beatitudes, these are the things which will become visible. Neither the cross, nor their membership in such a community betoken any merit of their own—the praise is due to God alone. If the good works were a galaxy of human virtues, we should then have to glorify the disciples, not God. But there is nothing for us to glorify in the disciple who bears the cross, or in the community whose light so shines because it stands visibly on the hill—only the Father which is in heaven can be praised for the "good works." It is by *seeing* the cross and the community beneath it that men come to believe in God. But that is the light of the Resurrection.

3

The Righteousness of Christ

Think not that I came to destroy the law or the prophets: I came not to destroy, but to fulfil. For verily I say unto you, Till heaven and earth pass away, one jot or one tittle shall in no wise pass away from the law, till all things be accomplished. Whosoever therefore shall break one of these least commandments, and shall teach men so, shall be called least in the kingdom of heaven: but whosoever shall do and teach them, he shall be called great in the kingdom of heaven. For I say unto you, that except your righteousness shall exceed the righteousness of the scribes and Pharisees, ye shall in no wise enter into the kingdom of heaven. (Matt. 5.17-20)

IT is not at all surprising that the disciples imagined that the law had been abrogated, when Jesus made promises like this. For these promises reversed all popular notions of right and wrong, and pronounced a blessing on all that was accounted worthless. Jesus spoke to his disciples and described them as men who now possessed all things through the sovereign grace of God, as heirs-apparent of the kingdom of heaven. They enjoy perfect communion with Christ, who had made all things new. They are the salt, the light, the city set on the hill. The old life is dead and done with. How tempting then to suppose that Jesus would give the old order its *coup de grâce* by repealing the law of the old covenant, and pronounce his followers free to enjoy the liberty of the Son of God! After all Jesus had said, the disciples might well have thought like Marcion, who accused the Jews of tampering with the text, and altered it to: "Think ye that I am come to fulfil the law and the prophets? I am not come to fulfil, but to destroy." Many others since Marcion have read and expounded this saying of Jesus as if that were what he said. But Jesus says: "You must not imagine that I have come to destroy the law or the prophets. . . ." And so saying he vindicates the authority of the law of the old covenant.

How is this to be understood? We know that Jesus is speaking to his own followers, to men who owe an exclusive allegiance to himself. He had allowed no law to act as a barrier to his fellowship with his disciples; we saw that when we were dealing with Luke 9.57 ff. Discipleship means adherence to Jesus Christ alone, and immediately. But now comes the surprise— the disciples are bound to the Old Testament law. This has a double significance. First, it means that adherence to the law is something quite different from the following of Christ, and, secondly, it means that any adherence to his person that disregards the law is equally removed from the following of him. It is, however, Jesus himself who points to the law those to whom he has granted his whole promise and his whole fellowship. Because it is their Lord who does this, they are bound to acknowledge the law. The question inevitably arises, Which is our final authority, Christ or the law? To which are we bound? Christ had said that no law was to be allowed to come between him and his disciples. Now he tells us that to abandon the law would be to separate ourselves from him. What exactly does he mean?

The law Jesus refers to is the law of the old covenant, not a new law, but the same law which he quoted to the rich young man and the lawyer when they wanted to know the revealed will of God. It becomes a new law only because it is Christ who binds his followers to it. For Christians, therefore, the law is not a "better law" than that of the Pharisees, but one and the same; every letter of it, every jot and tittle, must remain in force and be observed until the end of the world. But there is a "better righteousness" which is expected of Christians. Without it none can enter into the kingdom of heaven, for it is the indispensable condition of discipleship. None can have this better righteousness but those to whom Christ is speaking here, those whom he has called. The call of Christ, in fact Christ himself, is the *sine qua non* of this better righteousness.

Now we can see why up to now Jesus has said nothing about himself in the Sermon on the Mount. Between the disciples and the better righteousness demanded of them stands the Person of Christ, who came to fulfil the law of the old covenant. This is the fundamental presupposition of the whole Sermon on the Mount. Jesus manifests his perfect union with the will of God as revealed in the Old Testament law and prophets. He has in fact nothing to add to the commandments of God, except this, that he keeps them. He fulfils the law, and he tells us so himself, therefore it must be true. He fulfils the law down to the last iota. But that means that he must die, he alone understands the true nature of the law as God's law: the law is not itself God, nor is God the law. It was the error of Israel to put the law in God's place, to make the law their God and their God a law. The disciples were confronted with the opposite danger of denying the law its divinity altogether and divorcing God from his law. Both errors lead to the same result. By confounding God and the law, the Jews were trying to use the law to exploit the Law-giver: He was swallowed up in the law, and therefore no longer its Lord. By imagining that God and the law could be divorced from one another, the disciples were trying to exploit God by their possession of salvation. In both cases, the gift was confounded with the Giver: God was denied equally, whether it was with the help of the law, or with the promise of salvation.

Confronted with these twin errors, Jesus vindicates the divine authority of the law. God is its giver and its Lord, and only in personal communion with God is the law fulfilled. There is no fulfilment of the law apart from communion with God, and no communion with God apart from fulfilment of the law. To forget the first condition was the mistake of the Jews, and to forget the second the temptation of the disciples.

Jesus, the Son of God, who alone lives in perfect communion with him, vindicates the law of the old covenant by coming to fulfil it. He was the only Man who ever fulfilled the law, and therefore he alone can teach the law and its fulfilment aright. The disciples would naturally grasp that as soon as he told them, for they knew who he was. But the Jews could not grasp it as long as they refused to believe in him. It was thus only to be expected that they would reject his teaching on the law: to them it was blasphemy against God, because it was blasphemy against his law. Jesus, the champion of the true law, must suffer at the hands of the champions of the false law. He dies on the cross as a blasphemer, a transgressor of the law, because he has vindicated the true against the false.

The only way for him to fulfil the law is by dying a sinner's death on the cross. There he embodies in his person the perfect fulfilment of the law.

That is to say, Jesus Christ and he alone fulfils the law, because he alone lives in perfect communion with God. It is Jesus himself who comes between the disciples and the law, not the law which comes between Jesus and the disciples. They find their way to the law through the cross of Christ. Thus by pointing his disciples to the law which he alone fulfils, he forges a further bond between himself and them. He must needs reject the notion that men can cleave to him and be free from the law, for that spells enthusiasm, and so far from leading to adherence to Jesus, means libertarianism. But this allays the disciples' anxiety that adherence to the law would sever them from Jesus. Such an anxiety could only spring from that self-same error which cut off the Jews from God. Instead the disciples now learn that genuine adherence to Christ also means adherence to the law of God.

But if Jesus comes between the disciples and the law, he does so not to release them from the duties it imposes, but to validate his demand that they should fulfil it. Just because they are bound to him, they must obey the law as he does. The fact that Jesus has fulfilled the law down to the very last letter does not release them from the same obedience. The law is fulfilled, that is all. But it is precisely this which makes it properly valid for the first time. That is why he who obeys and teaches the law will be great in the kingdom of heaven. "*Do* and teach": we are reminded that it is possible to teach the law without fulfilling it, to teach it in such a way that it cannot be fulfilled. That sort of teaching has no warrant from Jesus. The law will be obeyed as certainly as he obeyed it himself. If men cleave to him who fulfilled the law and follow him, they will find themselves both teaching and fulfilling the law. Only the doer of the law can remain in communion with Jesus.

It is not the law which distinguishes the disciples from the Jews, but the "better righteousness." The righteousness of the disciples, we are told, exceeds that of the scribes. That is because it is something extraordinary and unusual. This is the first time we meet the word περισσεύειν, which is so important in verse 47. We must ask, how exactly does the righteousness of the Pharisees differ from that of the disciples? Certainly the Pharisees never imagined that the law must be taught but not obeyed: they knew their Bibles better than that! No, it was rather their ambition to be doers of the law. Their idea of righteousness was a direct, literal and practical fulfilment of the commandment, their ideal was to model their behaviour exactly on the demands of the law. Of course they knew that they could never realize that ideal, there was bound to be an excess which needed forgiveness of sins to cover it. Their obedience was never more than imperfect. With the disciple also righteousness could only take the form of obedience to the law. No one who failed to do the law could be accounted righteous. But the disciple had the advantage over the Pharisee in that his doing of the law is in fact perfect. How is such a thing possible? Because between the disciples and the law stands one who has perfectly fulfilled it, one with whom they live in communion. They are faced not with a law which has never yet been fulfilled, but with one whose demands have already been satisfied. The righteousness it demands is already there, the righteousness of Jesus which submits to the cross because that is what the law demands. This righteousness is therefore not a duty owed, but a perfect and truly personal communion with God, and Jesus not only posesses this righteousness, but is himself the personal embodiment of it. He *is* the righteousness of the disciples. By calling them he has admitted them to partnership with himself, and made them partakers of his righteousness in its fulness. That is what Jesus means when he prefaces his teaching on the "better righteousness" with reference to his own fulfilment of the law. Of course the righteousness of the disciples can never be a personal achievement; it is always a gift, which they received when they were called to follow him. In fact their righteousness consists precisely in their following him, and in the beatitudes the reward of the kingdom of heaven has been promised to it. It is a righteousness under the cross, it belongs only to the poor, the tempted, the hungry, the meek, the peacemakers, the persecuted—who endure their lot for the sake of Jesus; it is the visible righteousness of those who for the sake of Jesus are the light of the world and the city set on the hill. This is where the righteousness of the disciple exceeds that of the Pharisees; it is grounded solely upon the call to fellowship with him who alone fulfils the law. Their righteousness is righteousness indeed, for from henceforth they do the will of God and fulfil the law themselves. Again, it is not enough to teach the law of Christ, it must be *done*, otherwise it is no better than the old law. In what follows the disciples are told how to practise this righteousness of Christ. In a word, it means following him. It is the real and active faith in the righteousness of Christ. It is the new law, the law of Christ.

4

The Brother

Ye have heard that it was said to them of old time, Thou shalt not kill; and whosoever shall kill shall be in danger of the judgement: but I say unto you, that every one who is angry with his brother shall be in danger of the judgement; and whosoever shall say to his brother, Raca, shall be in danger of the council; and whosoever shall say, Thou fool, shall be in danger of the hell of fire. If therefore thou art offering thy gift at the altar, and there rememberest that thy brother hath aught against thee, leave there thy gift before the altar, and go thy way, first be reconciled to thy brother, and then come and offer thy gift. Agree with thine adversary quickly, whiles thou art with him in the way; lest haply the adversary deliver thee to the judge, and the judge deliver thee to the officer, and thou be cast into prison. Verily I say unto thee, Thou shalt by no means come out thence, till thou have paid the last farthing. (Matt. 5.21-26)

"But I say unto you"—Jesus sums up the whole purport of the law. All he has said so far makes it impossible to regard him here as a revolutionary, or as a rabbi pitting one opinion against another. On the contrary, Jesus is simply picking up the argument where he left off, and affirming his agreement with the law of the Mosaic covenant. But—and this is where he is at one with the law of God—he makes it perfectly clear that he, the Son of God, is the Author

and Giver of the law. Only those who apprehend the
law as the word of Christ are in a position to fulfil it.
The heresy of the Pharisees must be excluded at all
costs. Only by knowing Christ as the Giver and Ful-
filler of the law can we attain to a true knowledge of
the law. Christ has laid his hand on the law, and by
claiming it for his own, he brings it to fruition. But
while he is in perfect agreement with the law as such,
he declares war on all false interpretations of it, and
by honouring it he gives himself into the hands of its
false devotees.

The first law which Jesus commends to his disciples
is the one which forbids murder and entrusts their
brother's welfare to their keeping. The brother's life
is a divine ordinance, and God alone has power over
life and death. There is no place for the murderer
among the people of God. The judgement he passes
on others falls on the murderer himself. In this con-
text "brother" means more than "fellow-Christian":
for the follower of Jesus there can be no limit as to
who is his neighbour, except as his Lord decides. He
is forbidden to commit murder under pain of divine
judgement. For him the brother's life is a boundary
which he dare not pass. Even anger is enough to
overstep the mark, still more the casual angry word
(*Raca*), and most of all the deliberate insult of our
brother ("Thou fool").

Anger is always an attack on the brother's life, for
it refuses to let him live and aims at his destruction.
Jesus will not accept the common distinction between
righteous indignation and unjustifiable anger.[1] The
disciple must be entirely innocent of anger, because

---

[1] The addition εἰκῇ in the majority of MSS. (though not in
א and B) is the first attempt to mitigate the harshness of this
saying.

anger is an offence against both God and his neighbour. Every idle word which we think so little of be-
trays our lack of respect for our neighbour, and shows
that we place ourselves on a pinnacle above him and
value our own lives higher than his. The angry word
is a blow struck at our brother, a stab at his heart: it
seeks to hit, to hurt and to destroy. A deliberate insult is even worse, for we are then openly disgracing
our brother in the eyes of the world, and causing others
to despise him. With our hearts burning with hatred,
we seek to annihilate his moral and material existence.
We are passing judgement on him, and that is murder.
And the murderer will himself be judged.

When a man gets angry with his brother and swears
at him, when he publicly insults or slanders him, he
is guilty of murder and forfeits his relation to God.
He erects a barrier not only between himself and
his brother, but also between himself and God. He
no longer has access to him: his sacrifice, worship and
prayer are not acceptable in his sight. For the Christian, worship cannot be divorced from the service of
the brethren, as it was with the rabbis. If we despise
our brother our worship is unreal, and it forfeits
every divine promise. When we come before God with
hearts full of contempt and unreconciled with our
neighbours, we are, both individually and as a congregation, worshipping an idol. So long as we refuse
to love and serve our brother and make him an object
of contempt and let him harbour a grudge against
me or the congregation, our worship and sacrifice
will be unacceptable to God. Not just the fact that
I am angry, but the fact that there is somebody who
has been hurt, damaged and disgraced by me, who
"has a cause against me," erects a barrier between
me and God. Let us therefore as a Church examine

ourselves, and see whether we have not often enough wronged our fellow-men. Let us see whether we have tried to win popularity by falling in with the world's hatred, its contempt and its contumely. For if we do that we are murderers. Let the fellowship of Christ so examine itself to-day and ask whether, at the hour of prayer and worship, any accusing voices intervene and make its prayer vain. Let the fellowship of Christ examine itself and see whether it has given any token of the love of Christ to the victims of the world's contumely and contempt, any token of that love of Christ which seeks to preserve, support and protect life. Otherwise however liturgically correct our services are, and however devout our prayer, however brave our testimony, they will profit us nothing, nay rather, they must needs testify against us that we have as a Church ceased to follow our Lord. God will not be separated from our brother: he wants no honour for himself so long as our brother is dishonoured. God is the Father, the Father of our Lord Jesus Christ, who became the Brother of us all. Here is the final reason why God will not be separated from our brother. His only-begotten Son bore the shame and insults for his Father's glory. But the Father would not be separated from his Son, nor will he now turn his face from those whose likeness the Son took upon him, and for whose sake he bore the shame. The Incarnation is the ultimate reason why the service of God cannot be divorced from the service of man. He who says he loves God and hates his brother is a liar.

There is therefore only one way of following Jesus and of worshipping God, and that is to be reconciled with our brethren. If we come to hear the Word of God and receive the sacrament without first being reconciled with our neighbours, we shall come to

our own damnation. In the sight of God we are murderers. Therefore "go thy way, first be reconciled with
thy brother, and then come and offer thy gift." This
is a hard way, but it is the way Jesus requires if we
are to follow him. It is a way which brings much personal humiliation and insult, but it is indeed the way
to him, our crucified Brother, and therefore a way of
grace abounding. In Jesus the service of God and the
service of the least of the brethren were one. He went
his way and became reconciled with his brother and
offered himself as the one true sacrifice to his Father.

We are still living in the age of grace, for each of
us still has a brother, we are still "with him in the
way." The court of judgement lies ahead, and there
is still a chance for us to be reconciled with our
brother and pay our debt to him. The hour is coming
when we shall meet the judge face to face, and then
it will be too late. We shall then receive our sentence
and be made to pay the last farthing. But do we
realize that at this point our brother comes to us in
the guise not of law, but of grace? It is grace that we
are allowed to please our brother, and pay our debt
to him, it is grace that we are allowed to become
reconciled with him. In our brother we find grace before the seat of judgement.

Only he can speak thus to us, who as our Brother
has himself become our grace, our atonement, our deliverance from judgement. The humanity of the Son
of God grants us the gift of a brother. May the
disciples of Jesus think upon this grace aright!

To serve our brother, to please him, to allow him his
due and to let him live, is the way of self-denial, the
way of the cross. Greater love hath no man than this,
that a man lay down his life for his friends. That is the
love of the Crucified. Only in the cross of Christ do
we find the fulfilment of the law.

5

Woman

Ye have heard that it was said, Thou shalt not commit adultery: but I say unto you, that every one that looketh on a woman to lust after her hath committed adultery with her already in his heart. And if thy right eye causeth thee to stumble, pluck it out, and cast it from thee: for it is profitable for thee that one of thy members should perish, and not thy whole body be cast into hell. And if thy right hand causeth thee to stumble, cut it off, and cast it from thee: for it is profitable for thee that one of thy members should perish, and not thy whole body go into hell. It was said also, Whosoever shall put away his wife, let him give her a writing of divorcement: but I say unto you, that everyone that putteth away his wife, saving for the cause of fornication, maketh her an adulteress: and whosoever shall marry her when she is put away committeth adultery. (Matt. 5.27-32)

ADHERENCE TO Jesus allows no free rein to desire unless it be accompanied by love. To follow Jesus means self-renunciation and absolute adherence to him, and therefore a will dominated by lust can never be allowed to do what it likes. Even momentary desire is a barrier to the following of Jesus, and brings the whole body into hell, making us sell our heavenly birthright for a mess of pottage, and showing that we lack faith in him who will reward mortification with joy a hundredfold. Instead of trusting to the unseen, we prefer the tangible fruits of desire, and so we fall from the path of discipleship and lose touch with Jesus. Lust is impure because it is

35

unbelief, and therefore it is to be shunned. No sacrifice is too great if it enables us to conquer a lust which cuts us off from Jesus. Both eye and hand are less than Christ, and when they are used as the instruments of lust and hinder the whole body from the purity of discipleship, they must be sacrificed for the sake of him. The gain of lust are trivial compared with the loss it brings—you forfeit your body eternally for the momentary pleasure of eye or hand. When you have made your eye the instrument of impurity, you cannot see God with it. Surely, at this point we must make up our minds once and for all whether Jesus means his precepts to be taken literally or only figuratively, for here it is a matter of life or death. But the question is answered by the reaction of the disciples. Our natural inclination is to avoid a definite decision over this apparently crucial question. But the question is itself both wrong and wicked, and it does not admit of an answer. If we decided not to take it literally, we should be evading the seriousness of the commandment, and if on the other hand we decided it was to be taken literally, we should at once reveal the absurdity of the Christian position, and thereby invalidate the commandment. The fact that we receive no answer to the question only makes the commandment even more inescapable. We cannot evade the issue either way; we are placed in a position where there is no alternative but to obey. Jesus does not impose intolerable restrictions on his disciples, he does not forbid them to look at anything, but bids them look on him. If they do that he knows that their gaze will always be pure, even when they look upon a woman. So far from imposing on them an intolerable yoke of legalism, he succours them with the grace of the gospel.

Jesus does not enjoin his disciples to marry, but he does sanctify marriage according to the law by affirming its indissolubility and by prohibiting the innocent party from remarrying when the guilty partner has broken the marriage by adultery. This prohibition liberates marriage from selfish, evil desire, and consecrates it to the service of love, which is possible only in a life of discipleship. Jesus does not depreciate the body and its natural instincts, but he does condemn the unbelief which is so often latent in its desires. So far then from abolishing marriage, he sets it on a firmer basis and sanctifies it through faith. The disciple's exclusive adherence to Christ therefore extends even to his married life. Christian marriage is marked by discipline and self-denial. Christ is the Lord even of marriage. There is of course a difference between the Christian and the bourgeois conception of marriage, but Christianity does not therefore depreciate marriage, it sanctifies it.

It would appear that by affirming the indissolubility of marriage Jesus contradicts the law of the Old Testament. But there is another passage (Matt. 19.8) which shows that in fact he is at one with the law of Moses. There he says that divorce was permitted to the Israelites "for your hardness of heart"—in other words, it was to preserve them from worse excesses. The intention of the Old Testament law is the same as that of Jesus, to uphold the purity of marriage, and to see that it is exercised in faith in God. But purity or chastity is safeguarded amongst those who follow Jesus and share his life.

Being concerned exclusively with the perfect purity, that is to say, the chastity of his disciples, Jesus also approves of absolute celibacy for the sake of the kingdom of heaven. But he lays down no definite programme for his disciples, whether of celibacy or of marriage, only he delivers them from the perils of πορνεία (i.e. any sexual irregularity inside or outside of the married life). Such irregularity is a sin, not only against our own bodies, but against the Body of Christ (I Cor. 6.13-15). Even our bodies belong to Christ and have their part in the life of discipleship, for they are members of his Body. Jesus, the Son of God, bore a human body, and since we enjoy fellowship with that Body, fornication is a sin against Christ's own Body.

The body of Jesus was crucified. St. Paul, speaking of those who belong to Christ, says that they have crucified their body with its affections and lusts (Gal. 5.24). Here we have another instance of an Old Testament law finding its truest fulfilment in the crucified body of Jesus Christ. As they contemplate this body which was given for them, and as they share its life, the disciples receive strength for the chastity which Jesus requires.

6

Truthfulness

Again, ye have heard that it was said to them of old time, Thou shalt not forswear thyself, but shalt perform unto the Lord thine oaths: but I say unto you, Swear not at all; neither by the heaven, for it is the throne of God; nor by the earth, for it is the footstool of his feet; nor by Jerusalem, for it is the city of the great King. Neither shalt thou swear by thy head, for thou canst not make one hair white or black. But let your speech be, Yea, yea; Nay, nay: and whatsoever is more than these is of the evil one. (Matt. 5.33-37)

THE CHRISTIAN CHURCH has until now been strangely uncertain about the interpretation of this passage. Since the time of the primitive Church, commenators have oscillated between a rigorism which rejects every oath as a sin, and a more liberal position which rejects only frivolous oaths and downright perjury. In the early Church the commonest interpretation was that "perfect" Christians were forbidden to swear at all, but the weaker brethren were allowed to swear within certain limits. Augustine represents this latter point of view. He found himself in agreement with the teaching of Plato, the Pythagoreans, Epictetus, Marcus Aurelius, and other pagan philosophers, who maintained that oaths were beneath the dignity of gentlemen. In the Reformation Confessions it is expressly affirmed that there can be no question of

Jesus prohibiting oaths exacted by the state in a court of law. Were not such oaths expressly enjoined in the Old Testament? Jesus himself had sworn before a court of law, and St Paul frequently employs expressions of an oath-like character. Next to scriptural proof, the distinction between the spiritual and worldly realms was of decisive importance for the Reformers.

What is an oath? It is an appeal made to God in public, calling upon him to witness a statement made in connection with an event or fact, past, present or future. By means of the oath, men invoke the omniscient deity to avenge the truth. How can Jesus say that such an oath is "sin," "from the evil one," ἐκ τοῦ πονηροῦ, "satanic"? The answer is to be sought in his concern for complete truthfulness.

The very existence of oaths is a proof that there are such things as lies. If lying were unknown, there would be no need for oaths. Oaths are intended as a barrier against untruthfulness. But it goes further than that: for there, where alone the oath claims final truth, is space in life given to the lie, and it is granted a certain right of life. The Old Testament had expressed its condemnation of the lie by the use of the oath. But Jesus destroys the lie by forbidding oaths altogether. Here as there it is the same question, one and undivided, of the destruction of untruth in the life of the believer. The oath which the Old Testament set against the lie is seized by the lie itself and pressed into service. It is thus able through the oath to establish itself and to take the law into its own hands. So the lie must be seized by Jesus in the very place to which it flees, in the oath. Therefore the oath must go, since it is a protection for the lie.

There are two ways in which untruthfulness can

undermine the oath: either it may actually insinuate itself into the oath (perjury), or else disguise itself in the form of an oath by invoking some secular or divine power instead of the living God. When once the lie had entrenched itself behind the oath, there was no other way of ensuring complete truthfulness but by abolishing the oath altogether.

"Let your speech be Yea, yea, and Nay, nay." This is not to say that the disciples are no longer answerable to the omniscient God for every word they utter, it means that *every* word they utter is spoken in his presence, and not only those words which are accompanied by an oath. Hence they are forbidden to swear at all. Since they always speak the whole truth and nothing but the truth, there is no need for an oath, which would only throw doubt on the veracity of all their other statements. That is why the oath is "of the evil one." But a disciple must be a light even in his words.

It is clear that the only reason why Jesus prohibits the swearing of oaths lies in this concern for truthfulness. It also goes without saying that he admits no exceptions, however high the court of law may be. But at the same time it must be admitted that the abolition of oaths is in itself no guarantee that the truth will be told, indeed it may only lead to its concealment. No general rule can be laid down to enable us to decide where this is so, i.e. where an oath is desirable precisely in the interests of the truth; each case must be decided on its own merits. The Churches of the Reformation were convinced that every oath demanded by the state was covered by this exception. But it is questionable whether it is possible to lay down a general rule like that.

There is, however, no question that when such a

case appears to arise, an oath can only be sworn where all its implications are first made clear beyond all doubt. Secondly, a distinction must be drawn between oaths which apply to past or present facts, which are known, and oaths which pledge us with reference to the future. Since the profession of Christianity does not confer an infallible knowledge of the past, the invocation of almighty God will serve only to establish the integrity of his mind and conscience but not to confirm a statement which after all may be open to error. Moreover, since he is never lord of his own future, he will always be extremely cautious about giving a pledge (e.g. an oath of allegiance), for he is aware how dangerous it is to do so. And if his own future is outside his own control, how much more is the future of the authority which demands the oath of allegiance! For the sake of the truth, therefore, and for the sake of his following of Christ, he cannot swear such an oath without the proviso, "God willing." For the Christian no earthly obligation is absolutely binding, and any oath which makes an unconditional demand on him will for him be a lie which proceeds "from the evil one." In such a case the utmost an oath can do is to testify to the fact that the Christian is bound to the will of God alone, and that every other obligation is for the sake of Jesus conditional upon that will. If in a doubtful case this proviso is not explicitly stated or acknowledged, the oath cannot then be sworn, otherwise the Christian would be deceiving the authority. Let your speech, however, be: Yea, yea, Nay, nay.

The commandment of complete truthfulness is really only another name for the totality of discipleship. Only those who follow Jesus and cleave to him are living in complete truthfulness. Such men have nothing to hide from their Lord. Their life is revealed before him, Jesus has recognized them and led them into the way of truth. They cannot hide their sinfulness from Jesus, for they have not revealed themselves to Jesus, but he has revealed himself to them by calling them to follow him. At the moment of their call Jesus showed up their sin and made them aware of it. Complete truthfulness is only possible where sin has been uncovered, and forgiven by Jesus. Only those who are in a state of truthfulness through the confession of their sin to Jesus are not ashamed to tell the truth wherever it must be told. The truthfulness which Jesus demands from his followers is the self-abnegation which does not hide sin. Nothing is then hidden, everything is brought forth to the light of day.

In this question of truthfulness, what matters first and last is that a man's whole being should be exposed, his whole evil laid bare in the sight of God. But sinful men do not like this sort of truthfulness, and they resist it with all their might. That is why they persecute it and crucify it. It is only because we follow Jesus that we can be genuinely truthful, for then he reveals to us our sin upon the cross. The cross is God's truth about us, and therefore it is the only power which can make us truthful. When we know the cross we are no longer afraid of the truth. We need no more oaths to confirm the truth of our utterances, for we live in the perfect truth of God.

There is no truth towards Jesus without truth towards man. Untruthfulness destroys fellowship, but truth cuts false fellowship to pieces and establishes genuine brotherhood. We cannot follow Christ unless we live in revealed truth before God and man.

7

Revenge

Ye hath heard that it was said, An eye for an eye, and a
tooth for a tooth: but I say unto you, Resist not him that is
evil: but whosover smiteth thee on thy right cheek, turn to
him the other also. And if any man would go to law with
thee, and take away thy coat, let him have thy cloke also.
And whosoever shall compel thee to go one mile, go with
him twain. Give to him that asketh thee, and from him that
would borrow of thee turn not thou away. (Matt. 5.38-42)

JESUS CLASSES this saying about an eye
for an eye and a tooth for a tooth with the commandments which he has already quoted from the Old
Testament, for instance, the sixth commandment
against murder. He recognizes this saying, like the
sixth commandment, as the veritable law of God. This
law, like all the others, is not to be abrogated, but
fulfilled to the last iota. Jesus will not countenance
the modern practice of putting the decalogue on a
higher level than the rest of the Old Testament law.
For him the law of the Old Testament is a unity, and
he insists to his disciples that it must be fulfilled.

The followers of Jesus for his sake renounce every
personal right. He calls them blessed because they are
meek. If after giving up everything else for his sake
they still wanted to cling to their own rights, they
would then have ceased to follow him. This passage
therefore is simply an elaboration of the beatitudes.

44

In the Old Testament personal rights are protected by a divinely established system of retribution. Every evil must be requited. The aim of retribution is to establish a proper community, to convict and overcome evil and eradicate it from the body politic of the people of God. That is the purpose of the law which is maintained by retribution.

Jesus takes up this declaration of the divine will and affirms the power of retribution to convict and overcome evil and to ensure the fellowship of the disciples as the true Israel. By exercising the right kind of retribution evil is to be overcome and thus the true disciple will prove himself.

The right way to requite evil, according to Jesus, is not to resist it.

This saying of Christ removes the Church from the sphere of politics and law. The Church is not to be a national community like the old Israel, but a community of believers without political or national ties. The old Israel had been both—the chosen people of God *and* a national community, and it was therefore his will that they should meet force with force. But with the Church it is different: it has abandoned political and national status, and therefore it must patiently endure aggression. Otherwise evil will be heaped upon evil. Only thus can fellowship be established and maintained.

At this point it becomes evident that when a Christian meets with injustice, he no longer clings to his rights and defends them at all costs. He is absolutely free from possessions and bound to Christ alone. Again, his witness to this exclusive adherence to Jesus creates the only workable basis for fellowship, and leaves the aggressor for him to deal with.

The only way to overcome evil is to let it run itself

to a standstill because it does not find the resistance it is looking for. Resistance merely creates further evil and adds fuel to the flames. But when evil meets no opposition and encounters no obstacle but only patient endurance, its sting is drawn, and at last it meets an opponent which is more than its match. Of course this can only happen when the last ounce of resistance is abandoned, and the renunciation of revenge is complete. Then evil cannot find its mark, it can breed no further evil, and is left barren.

By willing endurance we cause suffering to pass. Evil becomes a spent force when we put up no resistance. By refusing to pay back the enemy in his own coin, and by preferring to suffer without resistance, the Christian exhibits the sinfulness of contumely and insult. Violence stands condemned by its failure to evoke counter-violence. When a man unjustly demands that I should give him my coat, I offer him my cloak also, and so counter his demand; when he requires me to go the other mile, I go willingly, and show up his exploitation of my service for what it is. To leave everything behind at the call of Christ is to be content with him alone, and to follow only him. By his willingly renouncing self-defence, the Christian affirms his absolute adherence to Jesus, and his freedom from the tyranny of his own ego. The exclusiveness of this adherence is the only power which can overcome evil.

We are concerned not with evil in the abstract, but with the evil *person*. Jesus bluntly calls the evil person evil. If I am assailed, I am not to condone or justify aggression. Patient endurance of evil does not mean a recognition of its rights. That is sheer sentimentality, and Jesus will have nothing to do with it. The shameful assault, the deed of violence and the

act of exploitation are still evil. The disciple must
realize this, and bear witness to it as Jesus did, just
because this is the only way evil can be met and overcome. The very fact that the evil which assaults him
is unjustifiable makes it imperative that he should not
resist it, but play it out and overcome it by patiently
enduring the evil person. Suffering willingly endured
is stronger than evil, it spells death to evil.

There is no deed on earth so outrageous as to justify
a different attitude. The worse the evil, the readier
must the Christian be to suffer; he must let the evil
person fall into Jesus' hands.

The Reformers offered a decisively new interpretation of this passage, and contributed a new idea of
paramount importance. They distinguished between
personal sufferings and those incurred by Christians
in the performance of duty as bearers of an office ordained by God, maintaining that the precept of non-
violence applies to the first but not to the second. In
the second case we are not only freed from obligation
to eschew violence, but if we want to act in a genuine
spirit of love we must do the very opposite, and meet
force with force in order to check the assault of evil.
It was along these lines that the Reformers justified
war and other legal sanctions against evil. But this
distinction between person and office is wholly alien
to the teaching of Jesus. He says nothing about that.
He addresses his disciples as men who have left all to
follow him, and the precept of non-violence applies
equally to private life and official duty. He is the Lord
of all life, and demands undivided allegiance. Furthermore, when it comes to practice, this distinction raises
insoluble difficulties. Am I ever acting only as a private person or only in an official capacity? If I am
attacked am I not at once the father of my children,

the pastor of my flock, and e.g. a government official? Am I not bound for that very reason to defend myself against every attack, for reason of responsibility to my office? And am I not also always an individual, face to face with Jesus, even in the performance of my official duties? Am I not therefore obliged to resist every attack just because of my responsibility for my office? Is it right to forget that the follower of Jesus is always utterly alone, always the individual, who in the last resort can only decide and act for himself? Don't we act most responsibly on behalf of those entrusted to our care if we act in this aloneness?

How then can the precept of Jesus be justified in the light of experience? It is obvious that weakness and defencelessness only invite aggression. Is then the demand of Jesus nothing but an impracticable ideal? Does he refuse to face up to realities—or shall we say, to the sin of the world? There may of course be a legitimate place for such an ideal in the inner life of the Christian community, but in the outside world such an ideal appears to wear the blinkers of perfectionism, and to take no account of sin. Living as we do in a world of sin and evil, we can have no truck with anything as impracticable as that.

Jesus, however, tells us that it is just *because* we live in the world, and just *because* the world is evil, that the precept of non-resistance must be put into practice. Surely we do not wish to accuse Jesus of ignoring the reality and power of evil! Why, the whole of his life was one long conflict with the devil. He calls evil evil, and that is the very reason why he speaks to his followers in this way. How is that possible?

If we took the precept of non-resistance as an ethical blueprint for general application, we should indeed be indulging in idealistic dreams: we should be dreaming of a utopia with laws which the world would never obey. To make non-resistance a principle for secular life is to deny God, by undermining his gracious ordinance for the preservation of the world. But Jesus is no draughtsman of political blueprints, he is the one who vanquished evil through suffering. It looked as though evil had triumphed on the cross, but the real victory belonged to Jesus. And the cross is the only justification for the precept of non-violence, for it alone can kindle a faith in the victory over evil which will enable men to obey that precept. And only such obedience is blessed with the promise that we shall be partakers of Christ's victory as well as of his sufferings.

The passion of Christ is the victory of divine love over the powers of evil, and therefore it is the only supportable basis for Christian obedience. Once again, Jesus calls those who follow him to share his passion. How can we convince the world by our preaching of the passion when we shrink from that passion in our own lives? On the cross Jesus fulfilled the law he himself established and thus graciously keeps his disciples in the fellowship of his suffering. The cross is the only power in the world which proves that suffering love can avenge and vanquish evil. But it was just this participation in the cross which the disciples were granted when Jesus called them to him. They are called blessed because of their visible participation in his cross.

8

The Enemy—the "Extraordinary"

Ye have heard that it was said, Thou shalt love thy neighbour, and hate thine enemy: but I say unto you, Love your
enemies, and pray for them that persecute you; that ye
may be sons of your Father which is in heaven: for he
maketh his sun to rise on the evil and the good, and sendeth
rain on the just and the unjust. For if ye love them that
love you, what reward have ye? do not even the publicans
the same? And if ye salute your brethren only, what do ye
more than others? do not even the Gentiles the same? Ye
therefore shall be perfect, as your heavenly Father is
perfect. (Matt. 5.43-48)

HERE, FOR the first time in the Sermon on
the Mount, we meet the word which sums up the
whole of its message, the word "love." Love is defined
in uncompromising terms as the love of our enemies.
Had Jesus only told us to love our brethren, we might
have misunderstood what he meant by love, but now
he leaves us in no doubt whatever as to his meaning.
   The enemy was no mere abstraction for the disciples. They knew him only too well. They came across
him every day. There were those who cursed them for
undermining the faith and transgressing the law.
There were those who hated them for leaving all they
had for Jesus' sake. There were those who insulted
and derided them for their weakness and humility.
There were those who persecuted them as prospective

dangerous revolutionaries and sought to destroy them. Some of their enemies were numbered among the champions of the popular religion, who resented the exclusive claim of Jesus. These last enjoyed considerable power and reputation. And then there was the enemy which would immediately occur to every Jew, the political enemy in Rome. Over and above all these, the disciples also had to contend with the hostility which invariably falls to the lot of those who refuse to follow the crowd, and which brought them daily mockery, derision and threats.

It is true that the Old Testament never explicitly bids us hate our enemies. On the contrary, it tells us more than once that we must love them (Ex. 23.4 f; Prov. 25.21 f; Gen. 45.1 ff; I Sam. 24.7; II Kings 6.22, etc.). But Jesus is not talking of ordinary enmity, but of that which exists between the People of God and the world. The wars of Israel were the only "holy wars" in history, for they were the wars of God against the world of idols. It is not this enmity which Jesus condemns, for then he would have condemned the whole history of God's dealings with his people. On the contrary, he affirms the old covenant. He is as concerned as the Old Testament with the defeat of the enemy and the victory of the People of God. No, the real meaning of this saying is that Jesus is again releasing his disciples from the political associations of the old Israel. From now on there can be no more wars of faith. The only way to overcome our enemy is by loving him.

To the natural man, the very notion of loving his enemies is an intolerable offence, and quite beyond his capacity: it cuts right across his ideas of good and evil. More important still, to man under the law, the idea of loving his enemies is clean contrary to the law of God, which requires men to sever all connection with their enemies and to pass judgement on them. Jesus, however, takes the law of God in his own hands and expounds its true meaning. The will of God, to which the law gives expression, is that men should defeat their enemies by loving them.

In the New Testament our enemies are those who harbour hostility against us, not those against whom we cherish hostility, for Jesus refuses to reckon with such a possibility. The Christian must treat his enemy as a brother, and requite his hostility with love. His behaviour must be determined not by the way others treat him, but by the treatment he himself receives from Jesus; it has only one source, and that is the will of Jesus.

By our enemies Jesus means those who are quite intractable and utterly unresponsive to our love, who forgive us nothing when we forgive them all, who requite our love with hatred and our service with derision, "For the love that I had unto them, lo, they now take my contrary part: but I give myself unto prayer" (Ps. 109.4). Love asks nothing in return, but seeks those who need it. And who needs our love more than those who are consumed with hatred and are utterly devoid of love? Who in other words deserves our love more than our enemy? Where is love more glorified than where she dwells in the midst of her enemies?

Christian love draws no distinction between one enemy and another, except that the more bitter our enemy's hatred, the greater his need of love. Be his enmity political or religious, he has nothing to expect from a follower of Jesus but unqualified love. In such love there is no inner discord between private person and official capacity. In both we are disciples of

Christ, or we are not Christians at all. Am I asked how this love is to behave? Jesus gives the answer: bless, do good, and pray for your enemies without reserve and without respect of persons.

"Love your enemies." The preceding commandment had spoken only of the passive endurance of evil; here Jesus goes further and bids us not only to bear with evil and the evil person patiently, not only to refrain from treating him as he treats us, but actively to engage in heart-felt love towards him. We are to serve our enemy in all things without hypocrisy and with utter sincerity. No sacrifice which a lover would make for his beloved is too great for us to make for our enemy. If out of love for our brother we are willing to sacrifice goods, honour and life, we must be prepared to do the same for our enemy. We are not to imagine that this is to condone his evil; such a love proceeds from strength rather than weakness, from truth rather than fear, and therefore it cannot be guilty of the hatred of another. And who is to be the object of such a love, if not those whose hearts are stifled with hatred?

"Bless them that persecute you." If our enemy cannot put up with us any longer and takes to cursing us, our immediate reaction must be to lift up our hands and bless him. Our enemies are the blessed of the Lord. Their curse can do us no harm. May their poverty be enriched with all the riches of God, with the blessing of him whom they seek to oppose in vain. We are ready to endure their curses so long as they redound to their blessing.

"Do good to them that hate you." We must love not only in thought and word, but in deed, and there are opportunities of service in every circumstance of daily life. "If thine enemy hunger, feed him; if he thirst,

give him to drink" (Rom. 12.20). As brother stands by brother in distress, binding up his wounds and soothing his pain, so let us show our love towards our enemy. There is no deeper distress to be found in the world, no pain more bitter than· our enemy's. Nowhere is service more necessary or more blessed than when we serve our enemies. "It is more blessed to give than to receive."

"Pray for them which despitefully use you and persecute you." This is the supreme demand. Through the medium of prayer we go to our enemy, stand by his side, and plead for him to God. Jesus does not promise that when we bless our enemies and do good to them they will not despitefully use and persecute us. They certainly will. But not even that can hurt or overcome us, so long as we pray for them. For if we pray for them, we are taking their distress and poverty, their guilt and perdition upon ourselves, and pleading to God for them. We are doing vicariously for them what they cannot do for themselves. Every insult they utter only serves to bind us more closely to God and them. Their persecution of us only serves to bring them nearer to reconciliation with God and to further the triumphs of love.

How then does love conquer? By asking not how the enemy treats her but only how Jesus treated her. The love for our enemies takes us along the way of the cross and into fellowship with the Crucified. The more we are driven along this road, the more certain is the victory of love over the enemy's hatred. For then it is not the disciple's own love, but the love of Jesus Christ alone, who for the sake of his enemies went to the cross and prayed for them as he hung there. In the face of the cross the disciples realized that they too were his enemies, and that he had overcome them by his love. It is this that opens the disciple's eyes, and enables him to see his enemy as a brother. He knows that he owes his very life to One, who though he was his enemy, treated him as a brother and accepted him, who made him his neighbour, and drew him into fellowship with himself. The disciple can now perceive that even his enemy is the object of God's love, and that he stands like himself beneath the cross of Christ. God asked us nothing about our virtues or our vices, for in his sight even our virtue was ungodliness. God's love sought out his enemies who needed it, and whom he deemed worthy of it. God loves his enemies—that is the glory of his love, as every follower of Jesus knows; through Jesus he has become a partaker in this love. For God allows his sun to shine upon the just and the unjust. But it is not only the earthly sun and the earthly rain: the "Sun of righteousness" and the rain of God's Word which are on the sinner, and reveal the grace of the Heavenly Father. Perfect, all-inclusive love is the act of the Father, it is also the act of the sons of God as it was the act of the only-begotten Son.

"This commandment, that we should love our enemies and forgo revenge will grow even more urgent in the holy struggle which lies before us and in which we partly have already been engaged for years. In it love and hate engage in mortal combat. It is the urgent duty of every Christian soul to prepare itself for it. The time is coming when the confession of the living God will incur not only the hatred and the fury of the world, for on the whole it has come to that already, but complete ostracism from 'human society,' as they call it. The Christians will be hounded from

place to place, subjected to physical assault, mal-
treatment and death of every kind. We are approach-
ing an age of widespread persecution. Therein lies the
true significance of all the movements and conflicts of
our age. Our adversaries seek to root out the Christian
Church and the Christian faith because they cannot
live side by side with us, because they see in every
word we utter and every deed we do, even when they
are not specifically directed against them, a condemnation of their own words and deeds. They are not far
wrong. They suspect too that we are indifferent to
their condemnation. Indeed they must admit that it is
utterly futile to condemn us. We do not reciprocate
their hatred and contention, although they would like
it better if we did, and so sink to their own level. And
how is the battle to be fought? Soon the time will
come when we shall pray, not as isolated individuals,
but as a corporate body, a congregation, a Church:
we shall pray in multitudes (albeit in relatively small
multitudes) and among the thousands and thousands
of apostates we shall loudly praise and confess the
Lord who was crucified and is risen and shall come
again. And what prayer, what confession, what hymn
of praise will it be? It will be the prayer of earnest
love for these very sons of perdition who stand around
and gaze at us with eyes aflame with hatred, and who
have perhaps already raised their hands to kill us. It
will be a prayer for the peace of these erring, devas-
tated and bewildered souls, a prayer for the same love
and peace which we ourselves enjoy, a prayer which
will penetrate to the depths of their souls and rend
their hearts more grievously than anything they can
do to us. Yes, the Church which is really waiting for
its Lord, and which discerns the signs of the times of
decision, must fling itself with its utmost power and

with the panoply of its holy life into this prayer of love." [1]

What is undivided love? Love which shows no special favour to those who love us in return. When we love those who love us, our brethren, our nation, our friends, yes, and even our own congregation, we are no better than the heathen and the publicans. Such love is ordinary and natural, and not distinctively Christian. We can love our kith and kin, our fellow-countrymen and our friends, whether we are Christians or not, and there is no need for Jesus to teach us that. But he takes that kind of love for granted, and in contrast asserts that we must love our enemies. Thus he shows us what *he* means by love, and the attitude we must display towards it.

How then do the disciples differ from the heathen? What does it really mean to be a Christian? Here we meet the word which controls the whole chapter, and sums up all we have heard so far. What make the Christian different from other men is the *"peculiar"* the περισσόν, the "extraordinary," the "unusual," that which is not "a matter of course." This is the quality whereby the better righteousness exceeds the righteousness of the scribes and Pharisees. It is "the more," the "beyond-all-that." The natural is τὸ αὐτὸ (one and the same) for heathen and Christian, the distinctive quality of the Christian life begins with the περισσόν. It is this quality which first enables us to see the natural in its true light. Where it is lacking, the peculiar graces of Christianity are absent. It cannot occur within the sphere of natural possibilities, but only when they are transcended. The περισσόν never merges into the τὸ αὐτὸ. That was the fatal mistake

---

[1] A. F. C. Vilmar, 1880.

of the false Protestant ethic which diluted Christian
love into patriotism, loyalty to friends and industrious-
ness, which in short, perverted the better righteousness into *justitia civilis*. Not in such terms as these
does Jesus speak. For him the hall-mark of the Christian is the "extraordinary." The Christian cannot live
at the world's level, because he must always remem-
ber the περισσόν.

What is the precise nature of the περισσόν? It is the
life described in the beatitudes, the life of the followers of Jesus, the light which lights the world, the city
set on the hill, the way of self-renunciation, of utter
love, of absolute purity, truthfulness and meekness.
It is unreserved love for our enemies, for the unloving
and the unloved, love for our religious, political and
personal adversaries. In every case it is the love which
was fulfilled in the cross of Christ. What is the
περισσόν? It is the love of Jesus Christ himself, who
went patiently and obediently to the cross—it is in fact
the cross itself. The cross is the differential of the
Christian religion, the power which enables the Christian to transcend the world and to win the victory.
The *passio* in the love of the Crucified is the supreme
expression of the "extraordinary" quality of the Christian life.

The "extraordinary" quality is undoubtedly identi-
cal with the light which shines before men and for
which they glorify the Father which is in heaven. It
cannot be hidden under a bushel, it must be seen of
men. The community of the followers of Jesus, the
community of the better righteousness, is the visible
community: it has left the world and society, and
counted everything but loss for the cross of Christ.

And how does this quality work out in practice?
The "extraordinary"—and this is the supreme scandal

—is something which the followers of Jesus *do*. It must be *done* like the better righteousness, and done so that all men can see it. It is not strict Puritanism, not some eccentric pattern of Christian living, but simple, unreflecting obedience to the will of Christ. If we make the "extraordinary" our standard, we shall be led into the *passio* of Christ, and in that its peculiar quality will be displayed. This activity itself is ceaseless suffering. In it the disciple endures the suffering of Christ. If this is not so, then *this* is not the activity of which Jesus speaks.

Hence the περισσόν is the fulfilment of the law, the keeping of the commandments. In Christ crucified and in his people the "extraordinary" becomes reality.

These men are the perfect, the men in whom the undivided love of the Heavenly Father is perfected. It was that love which gave the Son to die for us upon the cross, and it is by suffering in the fellowship of this cross that the followers of Jesus are perfected. The perfect are none other than the blessed of the beatitudes.

The Hidden Righteousness

Take heed that ye do not your righteousness before men, to be seen of them: else ye have no reward with your Father which is in heaven. When therefore thou doest alms sound not a trumpet before thee, as the hypocrites do in the synagogues and in the streets, that they may have glory of men. Verily I say unto you, They have received their reward. But when thou doest alms, let not thy left hand know what thy right hand doeth: that thine alms may be in secret: and thy Father which seeth in secret shall recompense thee. (Matt. 6.1-4)

IN CHAPTER 5 we were told how the disciple community is essentially visible in character, and how its visibility culminates in the περισσόν. We saw that the hall-mark of Christianity is our separation from the world, our transcendence of its standards, and our extraordinariness. The next chapter takes up the theme of the περισσόν, and lays bare its ambiguity. How easy it would be for the disciples to misinterpret it! We can well imagine them saying: "Now we must set to work and build the kingdom of heaven on earth"—and in so doing they would ignore and perhaps even overthrow the established order of things. They might adopt an attitude of indifference to this present age, like the enthusiasts, and try to realize the extraordinary quality of the age to come in a visible institution. Their ideal would then be to withdraw radically and uncompromisingly from the world and by means of force to set up a Christian order more compatible with their following of Christ and more in accordance with his extraordinary demand. There was an obvious temptation to mistake Christ's work for a commendation of a new, however novel, free and inspiring, pattern for pious living. How eagerly would the religious embrace a life of poverty, truthfulness and suffering, if only they might thereby satisfy their yearning not only to believe, but to see with their own eyes! One might have been prepared to move the distinctions between the two a little, so that a pious pattern of life and obedience towards God's Word might come a little closer together, so that in the end you could really not tell one from the other. After all, they could argue, they were doing it all for the supreme cause, the realization of the "extraordinary."

Others on the other hand would be waiting to hear what Jesus had to say about the "extraordinary," only to pounce upon him with all their fury. Here at last, they would say, the fanatic, the enthusiastic revolutionary has come out in his true colours. Now we know he wants to turn the whole world upside down and bids his disciples leave the world and build a new one. Is *this* obedience to the word of the Old Testament? Is it not rather the most glaring example of self-righteousness? Does not Jesus know that all he demands is bound to come to grief because of the world's sin? Does he not know the manifest laws of God given so that sin might be banished? Does it not prove him a victim of spiritual pride, always the first sign of fanaticism? No, they would say, genuine obedience and humility are only to be found in the

ordinary, the commonplace, and the hidden. Had Jesus
urged his disciples to return to their own kith and kin,
back to duty and calling, back to the obedience of the
law as the scribes expounded it, they would then have
known that he was devout, humble and obedient. He
would then have given his disciples an inspiring in-
centive to deeper devotion and stricter obedience. He
would have taught what the scribes knew already,
what they would gladly have heard him emphasize in
his preaching, namely that true devotion and righteousness consist not merely in outward behaviour,
but in the disposition of the heart, and conversely not
only in the disposition of the heart, but also in concrete action. That would have been just the kind of
"better righteousness" the people needed, and one
which nobody could have gainsaid. But now Jesus had
lost his chance. He had stepped forth not as a humble
teacher, but as an arrogant fanatic. Fanatics of course
have always known the secret of kindling the enthusiasm of men, especially the noblest and best of them.
Did not the doctors of the law know that for all its
nobility the heart of man still spoke with the voice
of the flesh? Did they now know themselves what
power even pious flesh could have over a man? The
"extraordinary" was simply the spontaneous work of
devotion and piety. It was the assertion of human
freedom against unreflecting obedience to the command of God, the illegitimate self-justification of man,
which the law does not permit; the lawless self-sanc-
tification which the law was bound to condemn; free
service to God as opposed to bounden duty, the destruction of the Church of God, the denial of faith,
blasphemy against the law and against God himself.
. . . If the law had its way Jesus would be put to
death for teaching the "extraordinary."

And how does Jesus answer these objections? He says: "Take heed that ye do not your righteousness befóre men, to be seen of them." The call to the "extraordinary" is the inevitable risk men must take when they follow Christ. And therefore Jesus warns us to take heed. He calls a halt to the innocent spontaneous joy we get from making our Christianity visible. He calls us to reflect on what we are doing.

The disciples are told that they can possess the "extraordinary" only so long as they are reflective: they must beware how they use it, and never fulfil it simply for its own sake, or for the sake of ostentation. The better righteousness of the disciples must have a motive which lies beyond itself. Of course it has to be visible, but they must take care that it does not become visible simply for the sake of becoming visible. There are of course proper grounds for insisting on the visible nature of Christian discipleship, but the visibility is never an end in itself; and if it becomes so we have lost sight of our primary aim, which is to follow Jesus. And, having once done that, we should never be able to carry on again where we had left off; we should have to begin all over again at the beginning. And that would bring it home to us that we were no true disciples. We are therefore confronted with a paradox. Our activity must be visible, but never be done for the sake of making it visible. "Let your light so shine before men" (5.16) and yet: Take care that you hide it! There is a pointed contrast between chapters 5 and 6. That which is visible must also be hidden. The awareness on which Jesus insists is intended to prevent us from reflecting on our extraordinary position. We have to take heed that we do not take heed of our own righteousness. Otherwise the "extraordinary" which we achieve will not be that which comes from following Christ, but that which springs from our own will and desire.

How is this paradox to be resolved? The first question to ask is: From whom are we to hide the visibility of our discipleship? Certainly not from other men, for we are told to let them see our light. No. We are to hide it from *ourselves.* Our task is simply to keep on following, looking only to our Leader who goes on before, taking no notice of ourselves or of what we are doing. We must be unaware of our own righteousness, and see it only in so far as we look unto Jesus; then it will seem not extraordinary, but quite ordinary and natural. Thus we hide the visible from ourselves in obedience to the word of Jesus. If the "extraordinary" were important for its own sake, we should, like fanatics, be relying on our own fleshly strength and power, whereas the disciple of Jesus acts simply in obedience to his Lord. That is, he regards the "extraordinary" as the natural fruit of obedience. According to the word of Jesus it cannot be otherwise: the Christian is a light unto the world, not because of any quality of his own, but only because he follows Christ and looks solely to him. But precisely because the Christian life is of its very nature extraordinary, it is at the same time ordinary, natural, and *hidden.* If not, it is not the Christian life at all, it is not obedience to the will of Jesus Christ.

Secondly, we have to ask how the visible and the invisible aspects of discipleship can be combined, and how the same life can be both visible and hidden. To answer this question, all we need to do is to go back to chapter 5, where the extraordinary and the visible are defined as the cross of Christ beneath which the disciples stand. The cross is at once the necessary, the hidden and the visible—it is the "extraordinary."

Thirdly, we have to ask how the contradiction between the fifth and the sixth chapters is to be resolved.
The answer lies in the meaning of discipleship. It
means an exclusive adherence to him, and that implies
first, that the disciple looks only to his Lord and follows him. If he looked only at the extraordinary
quality of the Christian life, he would no longer be
following Christ. For the disciple this extraordinary
quality consists solely in the will of the Lord, and
when he seeks to do that will he knows that there is no
other alternative, and that what he does is the only
natural thing to do.

All that the follower of Jesus has to do is to make
sure that his obedience, following and love are entirely spontaneous and unpremeditated. If you do
good, you must not let your left hand know what
your right hand is doing, you must be quite unconscious of it. Otherwise you are simply displaying your
own virtue, and not that which has its source in Jesus
Christ. Christ's virtue, the virtue of discipleship, can
only be accomplished so long as you are entirely unconscious of what you are doing. The genuine work
of love is always a hidden work. Take heed therefore
that you know it not, for only so is it the goodness of
God. If we want to know our own goodness or love,
it has already ceased to be love. We must be unaware
even of our love for our enemies. After all, when we
love them they are no longer our enemies. This voluntary blindness in the Christian (which is really sight
illuminated by Christ) is his certainty, and the fact
that his life is hidden from his sight is the ground
of his assurance.

Thus hiddenness has its counterpart in manifestation. For there is nothing hidden that shall not be
revealed. For our God is a God unto whom all hearts

are open, and from whom no secrets are hid. God will show us the hidden and make it visible. Manifestation is the appointed reward for hiddenness, and the only question is where we shall receive it and who will give it us. If we want publicity in the eyes of men we have our reward. In other words, it is immaterial whether the publicity we want is the grosser kind, which all can see, or the more subtle variety which we can only see ourselves. If the left hand knows what the right hand is doing, if we become conscious of our hidden virtue, we are forging our own reward, instead of that which God had intended to give us in his own good time. But if we are content to carry on with our life hidden from our eyes, we shall receive our reward openly from God. But what kind of love is this that is so unaware of itself that it can be hidden until the day of judgement? The answer is obvious. Because love is hidden it cannot be a visible virtue or a habit which can be acquired. Take heed, it says, that you do not exchange true love for an amiable virtuousness, a human "quality." Genuine love is always self-forgetful in the true sense of the word. But if we are to have it, our old man must die with all his virtues and qualities, and this can only be done where the disciple forgets self and clings solely to Christ. When Jesus said: "Let not thy left hand know what thy right hand doeth," he was sounding the death-knell of the old man. Once again, who can live a life which combines chapters 5 and 6? Only those who have died after the old man through Christ, and are given a new life by following him and having fellowship with him. Love, in the sense of spontaneous, unreflective action, spells the death of the old man. For man recovers his true nature in the righteousness of Christ and in his fellow-man. The love of Christ crucified, who delivers our old man to death, is the love which lives in those who follow him. "I live; yet no longer I, but Christ liveth in me" (Gal. 2.20). Henceforth the Christian finds himself only in Christ and in his brethren.

10

The Hiddenness of Prayer

And when ye pray, ye shall not be as the hypocrites: for they love to stand and pray in the synagogues and in the corners of the streets, that they may be seen of men. Verily I say unto you, They have received their reward. But thou, when thou prayest, enter into thine inner chamber, and having shut thy door, pray to thy Father which is in secret, and thy Father which seeth in secret shall recompense thee. And in praying use not vain repetitions, as the Gentiles do: for they think that they shall be heard for their much speaking. Be not therefore like unto them: for your Father knoweth what things ye hath need of, before ye ask him. (Matt. 6.5-8)

JESUS TEACHES his disciples to pray. What does this mean? It means that prayer is by no means an obvious or natural activity. It is the expression of a universal human instinct, but that does not justify it in the sight of God. Even where prayer is cultivated with discipline and perseverance it can still be profitless and void of God's blessing. The disciples are permitted to pray because Jesus tells them they may— and he knows the Father. He promises that God will hear them. That is to say, the disciples pray only because they are followers of Christ and have fellowship with him. Only those who, like them, adhere to Jesus have access to the Father through him. All

Christian prayer is directed to God through a Mediator, and not even prayer affords direct access to the Father. Only through Jesus Christ can we find the Father in prayer. Christian prayer presupposes faith, that is, adherence to Christ. He is the one and only Mediator of our prayers. We pray at his command, and to that word Christian prayer is always bound.

We pray to God because we believe in him through Jesus Christ; that is to say, our prayer can never be an entreaty to God, for we have no need to come before him in that way. We are privileged to know that he knows our needs before we ask him. This is what gives Christian prayer its boundless confidence and its joyous certainty. It matters little what form of prayer we adopt or how many words we use, what matters is the faith which lays hold on God and touches the heart of the Father who knew us long before we came to him.

Genuine prayer is never "good works," an exercise or a pious attitude, but it is always the prayer of a child to a Father. Hence it is never given to self-display, whether before God, ourselves, or other people. If God were ignorant of our needs, we should have to think out beforehand *how* we should tell him about them, *what* we should tell him, and whether we should tell him or not. Thus faith, which is the mainspring of Christian prayer, excludes all reflection and premeditation.

Prayer is the supreme instance of the hidden character of the Christian life. It is the antithesis of self-display. When men pray, they have ceased to know themselves, and know only God whom they call upon. Prayer does not aim at any direct effect on the world; it is addressed to God alone, and is therefore the perfect example of undemonstrative action.

Of course there is a danger even here. Prayer of this kind can seek self-display, it can seek to bring to light that which is hidden. This may happen in public prayer, which sometimes (though not often nowadays) degenerates into an empty noise. But there is no difference; it is even more pernicious if I turn myself into a spectator of my own prayer performance, if I am giving a show for my own benefit. I may enjoy myself just like a pleased spectator or I may catch myself praying and feel strange and ashamed. The publicity of the market place affords only a more naïve form than the publicity which I am providing for myself. I can lay on a very nice show for myself even in the privacy of my own room. That is the extent to which we can distort the word of Jesus. The publicity which I am looking for is then provided by the fact that I am the one who at the same time prays and looks on. I am listening to my own prayer and thus I am answering my own prayer. Not being content to wait for God to answer our prayer and show us in his own time that he has heard us, we provide our own answer. We take note that we have prayed suitably well, and this substitutes the satisfaction of answered prayer. We have our reward. Since we have heard ourselves, God will not hear us. Having contrived our own reward of publicity, we cannot expect God to reward us any further.

Where is the innermost chamber Jesus is thinking of where I can hide, if I cannot be sure of myself? How can I lock it so well that no audience spoils the anonymity of prayer and thus robs me of the reward of hidden prayer? How are we to be protected from ourselves, and our own premeditations? How are we to drive out reflection by reflecting? The only way is by mortifying our own wills which are always obtruding themselves. And the only way to do this is by letting Christ alone reign in our hearts, by surrendering our wills completely to him, by living in fellowship with Jesus and by following him. Then we can pray that his will may be done, the will of him who knows our needs before we ask. Only then is our prayer certain, strong and pure. And then prayer is really and truly *petition*. The child asks of the Father whom he knows. Thus the essence of Christian prayer is not general adoration, but definite, concrete petition. The right way to approach God is to stretch out our hands and ask of One who we know has the heart of a Father.

True prayer is done in secret, but this does not rule out the fellowship of prayer altogether, however clearly we may be aware of its dangers. In the last resort it is immaterial whether we pray in the open street or in the secrecy of our chambers, whether briefly or lengthily, in the Litany of the Church, or with the sigh of one who knows not what he should pray for. True prayer does not depend either on the individual or the whole body of the faithful, but solely upon the knowledge that our heavenly Father knows our needs. That makes God the sole object of our prayers, and frees us from a false confidence in our own prayerful efforts.

After this manner therefore pray ye: Our Father which art in heaven, Hallowed be thy name. Thy kingdom come. Thy will be done, as in heaven, so on earth. Give us this day our daily bread. And forgive us our debts, as we also have forgiven our debtors. And bring us not into temptation, but deliver us from the evil one. For if ye forgive not men their trespasses, neither will your Father forgive your trespasses. (Matt. 6.9-15)

Jesus told his disciples not only *how* to pray, but also *what* to pray. The Lord's Prayer is not merely the pattern prayer, it is the way Christians *must* pray. If they pray this prayer, God will certainly hear them. The Lord's Prayer is the quintessence of prayer. A disciple's prayer is founded on and circumscribed by it. Once again Jesus does not leave his disciples in ignorance; he teaches them the Lord's Prayer and so leads them to a clear understanding of prayer.

"Our Father which art in heaven." The disciples call upon the heavenly Father as a corporate body, they call upon a Father who already knows his children's needs. The call of Jesus binds them into a brotherhood. In Jesus they have apprehended the loving-kindness of the Father. In the name of the Son of God they are privileged to call God Father. They are on earth, and their Father is in heaven, He looks down on them from above, and they lift up their eyes to him.

"Hallowed be thy name." God's name of Father, as it has been revealed to the disciples in Jesus Christ, shall be kept holy among them. In this name the whole content of the gospel is embraced. May God protect his holy gospel from being obscured and profaned by false doctrine and unholiness of living, and may he ever make known his holy name to the disciples in Jesus Christ. May he enable all preachers to proclaim the pure gospel of saving grace, defend us against the tempters, and convert the enemies of his name!

"Thy kingdom come." In Jesus Christ his followers have witnessed the kingdom of God breaking in on earth. They have seen Satan crushed and the powers of the world, sin and death broken. The kingdom of God is still exposed to suffering and strife. The little flock has a share in that tribulation. They stand under the sovereignty of God in the new righteousness, but

in the midst of persecution. God grant that the kingdom of Jesus Christ may grow in his Church on earth,
God hasten the end of the kingdoms of this world,
and establish his own kingdom in power and glory!

"Thy will be done, as in heaven so on earth." In
fellowship with Jesus his followers have surrendered
their own wills completely to God's, and so they pray
that God's will may be done throughout the world.
No creature on earth shall defy him. But the evil will
is still alive even in the followers of Christ, it still
seeks to cut them off from fellowship with him; and
that is why they must also pray that the will of God
may prevail more and more in their hearts every day
and break down all defiance. In the end the whole
world must bow before that will, worshipping and
giving thanks in joy and tribulation. Heaven and earth
shall be subject to God.

God's name, God's kingdom, God's will must be the
primary object of Christian prayer. Of course it is
not as if God needed our prayers, but they are the
means by which the disciples become partakers in
the heavenly treasure for which they pray. Furthermore, God uses their prayers to hasten the coming
of the End.

"Give us this day our daily bread." As long as the
disciples are on earth, they should not be ashamed to
pray for their bodily needs. He who created men on
earth will keep and preserve their bodies. It is not
God's will that his creation should be despised. The
disciples are told to ask for bread not only for themselves but for all men on the earth, for all men are
their brethren. The disciples realize that while it is a
fruit of the earth, bread really comes down from
above as the gift of God alone. That is why they have
to ask for it before they take it. And since it is the

bread of God, it is new every day. They do not ask to lay up a store for the future, but are satisfied with what God gives them day by day. Through that bread their lives are spared a little longer, that they may enjoy life in fellowship with Jesus, praising and thanking him for his loving-kindness. This petition is a test of their faith, for it shows whether they believe that all things work together for good to them that love God.

"Forgive us our debts, as we also forgive our debtors." Every day Christ's followers must acknowledge and bewail their guilt. Living as they do in fellowship with him, they ought to be sinless, but in practice their life is marred daily with all manner of unbelief, sloth in prayer, lack of bodily discipline, self-indulgence of every kind, envy, hatred and ambition. No wonder that they must pray daily for God's forgiveness. But God will only forgive them if they forgive one another with readiness and brotherly affection. Thus they bring all their guilt before God and pray as a body for forgiveness. God forgive not merely *me my* debts, but *us ours.*

"Lead us not into temptation." Many and diverse are the temptations which beset the Christian. Satan attacks him on every side, if haply he might cause him to fall. Sometimes the attack takes the form of a false sense of security, and sometimes of ungodly doubt. But the disciple is conscious of his weakness, and does not expose himself unnecessarily to temptation in order to test the strength of his faith. Christians ask God not to put their puny faith to the test, but to preserve them in the hour of temptation.

"But deliver us from evil." The last petition is for deliverance from evil and for the inheritance of the kingdom of heaven. It is a prayer for a holy death and for the deliverance of the Church in the day of judgement.

"For thine is the kingdom. . . ." The disciples are renewed in their assurance that the kingdom is God's by their fellowship in *Jesus Christ, on whom depends the fulfilment of all their prayers.* In him God's name is hallowed, his kingdom comes and his will is done. For his sake the disciples are preserved in body and receive forgiveness of sin, in his strength they are preserved in all times of temptation, in his power they are delivered and brought to eternal life. His is the kingdom and the power and the glory for ever and ever in the unity of the Father. That is the assurance the disciples have.

As a summing up Jesus emphasizes once more that everything depends on forgiveness of sin of which the disciples may only partake within the fellowship of sinners.

11

The Hiddenness of the
Devout Life

Moreover when ye fast, be not, as the hypocrites, of a sad countenance: for they disfigure their faces, that they may be seen of men to fast. Verily I say unto you, They have received their reward. But thou, when thou fastest, anoint thy head, and wash thy face; that thou be not seen of men to fast, but of thy Father which is in secret: and thy Father, which seeth in secret, shall recompense thee. (Matt. 6.16-18)

JESUS TAKES it for granted that his disciples will observe the pious custom of fasting. Strict exercise of self-control is an essential feature of the Christian's life. Such customs have only one purpose —to make the disciples more ready and cheerful to accomplish those things which God would have done. Fasting helps to discipline the self-indulgent and slothful will which is so reluctant to serve the Lord, and it helps to humiliate and chasten the flesh. By practising abstemiousness we show the world how different the Christian life is from its own. If there is no element of asceticism in our lives, if we give free rein to the desires of the flesh (taking care of course to keep within the limits of what seems permissible to the world), we shall find it hard to train for the service of Christ. When the flesh is satisfied it is hard to pray with cheerfulness or to devote oneself to a life of service which calls for much self-renunciation.

So the Christian needs to observe a strict exterior discipline. But we are not to imagine that that alone will crush the will of the flesh, or that there is any way of mortifying our old man other than by faith in Jesus. The real difference in the believer who follows Christ and has mortified his will and died after the old man in Christ, is that he is more clearly aware than other men of the rebelliousness and perennial pride of the flesh, he is conscious of his sloth and self-indulgence and knows that his arrogance must be eradicated. Hence there is a need for daily self-discipline. It is always true of the disciple that the spirit is willing but the flesh is weak, and he must therefore "watch and pray." The spirit knows the right way, and desires to follow it, but the flesh lacks courage and finds it too hard, too hazardous and wearisome, and so it stifles the voice of the spirit. The spirit assents when Jesus bids us love our enemies, but flesh and blood are too strong and prevent our carrying it out. Therefore we have to practise strictest daily discipline; only so can the flesh learn the painful lesson that it has no rights of its own. Regular daily prayer is a great help here, and so is daily meditation on the Word of God, and every kind of bodily discipline and asceticism.

The flesh resists this daily humiliation, first by a frontal attack, and later by hiding itself under the words of the spirit (i.e. in the name of "evangelical liberty"). We claim liberty from all legal compulsion, from self-martyrdom and mortification, and play this off against the proper evangelical use of discipline and asceticism; we thus excuse our self-indulgence and irregularity in prayer, in meditation and in our bodily life. But the contrast between our behaviour and the word of Jesus is all too painfully evident. We forget that discipleship means estrangement from the world, and we forget the real joy and freedom which are the outcome of a devout rule of life. As soon as a Christian recognizes that he has failed in his service, that his readiness has become feeble, and that he has sinned against another's life and become guilty of another's guilt, that all his joy in God has vanished and that his capacity for prayer has quite gone, it is high time for him to launch an assault upon the flesh, and prepare for better service by fasting and prayer (Luke 2.37; 4.2; Mark 9.29; I Cor. 7.5). Any objection that asceticism is wrong, and that all we need is faith, is quite beside the point; it is cruel to suggest such a thing, and it is no help to us at all. When all is said and done, the life of faith is nothing if not an unending struggle of the spirit with every available weapon against the flesh. How is it possible to live the life of faith when we grow weary of prayer, when we lose our taste for reading the Bible, and when sleep, food and sensuality deprive us of the joy of communion with God?

Asceticism means voluntary suffering: it is *passio activa* rather than *passiva*, and it is just there that the danger lies. There is always a danger that in our asceticism we shall be tempted to imitate the sufferings of Christ. This is a pious but godless ambition, for beneath it there always lurks the notion that it is possible for us to step into Christ's shoes and suffer as he did and kill the old Adam. We are then presuming to undertake that bitter work of eternal redemption which Christ himself wrought for us. The motive of asceticism was more limited—to equip us for better service and deeper humiliation. But it can only do that so long at is takes the suffering of Christ as its basis; if not, it degenerates into a dreadful parody of the Lord's own passion. Our whole motive now becomes a desire for ostentation. We want other people to see our achievements and to be put to shame. Our asceticism has now become the way to salvation. Such publicity gives it the reward it seeks.

"Anoint thine head and wash thy face." Even this might become an occasion for a still subtler form of self-glorification or enjoyment. But that would be to miss the point and make of it a mere pretence. Jesus, however, bids his disciples to persevere in the practices of humiliation, but not to force them on other people as a rule or regulation. They must rejoice and give thanks for the privilege of remaining in the service of their Lord. Jesus does not mean that a smile on the face it to be a sort of stereotyped expression of Christianity; he is referring rather to the proper hiddenness of Christian behaviour, to that humility which is wholly unselfconscious, even as the eye can see other people but can never see itself. Such hiddenness will one day be made manifest, but that will be God's doing, not ours.

12
The Simplicity of the
Carefree Life

Lay not up for yourselves treasures upon the earth, where
moth and rust doth consume, and where thieves break
through and steal: but lay up for yourselves treasures in
heaven, where neither moth nor rust doth consume, and
where thieves do not break through nor steal: for where
thy treasure is, there will thy heart be also. The lamp of
the body is the eye: if therefore thine eye be single, thy
whole body shall be full of light. But if thine eye be evil,
thy whole body shall be full of darkness. If therefore the
light that is in thee be darkness, how great is the darkness!
No man can serve two masters: for either he will hate the
one and love the other; or else he will hold to one, and
despise the other. Ye cannot serve God and mammon.
(Matt. 6.19-24)

THE LIFE of discipleship can only be
maintained so long as nothing is allowed to come between Christ and ourselves—neither the law, nor
personal piety, nor even the world. The disciple always looks only to his master, never to Christ *and* the
law, Christ *and* religion, Christ *and* the world. He
avoids all such notions like the plague. Only by following Christ alone can he preserve a single eye. His eye
rests wholly on the light that comes from Christ, and
has no darkness or ambiguity in it. As the eye must

be single, clear and pure in order to keep light in the body, as hand and foot can receive light from no other source save the eye, as the foot stumbles and the hand misses its mark when the eye is dim, as the whole body is in darkness when the eye is blind; so the follower of Christ is in the light only so long as he looks simply to Christ and at nothing else in the world. Thus the heart of the disciple must be set upon Christ alone. If the eye sees an object which is not there, the whole body is deceived. If the heart is devoted to the mirage of the world, to the creature instead of the Creator, the disciple is lost.

Worldly possessions tend to turn the hearts of the disciples away from Jesus. What are we really devoted to? That is the question. Are our hearts set on earthly goods? Do we try to combine devotion to them with loyalty to Christ? Or are we devoted exclusively to him? The light of the body is the eye, and the light of the Christian is his heart. If the eye be dark, how great is the darkness of the body! But the heart is dark when it clings to earthly goods, for then, however urgently Jesus may call us, his call fails to find access to our hearts. Our hearts are closed, for they have already been given to another. As the light cannot penetrate the body when the eye is evil, so the word of Jesus cannot penetrate the disciple's heart so long as it is closed against it. The word is choked like the seed which was sown among thorns, choked "with cares and riches and pleasures of this life" (Luke 8.14).

The singleness of eye and heart corresponds to that "hiddenness" which knows nothing but the call and word of Christ, and which consists in perfect fellowship with him. How can the disciple have dealings with earthly goods and yet preserve this singleness of heart? Jesus does not forbid the possession of property in itself. He was man, he ate and drank like his disciples, and thereby sanctified the good things of life. These necessities, which are consumed in use and which meet the legitimate requirements of the body, are to be used by the disciple with thankfulness.

> *We walk as pilgrims through the earth,*
> *With empty hands, bereft and bare;*
> *To gather wealth were little worth—*
> *'Twould only burden life the more.*
>
> *If men will go the way to death,*
> *With them we will part company;*
> *For God will give us all we need*
> *To cover our necessity.*
>
> (TERSTEEGEN)

Earthly goods are given to be used, not to be collected. In the wilderness God gave Israel the manna every day, and they had no need to worry about food and drink. Indeed, if they kept any of the manna over until the next day, it went bad. In the same way, the disciple must receive his portion from God every day. If he stores it up as a permanent possession, he spoils not only the gift, but himself as well, for he sets his heart on his accumulated wealth, and makes it a barrier between himself and God. Where our treasure is, there is our trust, our security, our consolation and our God.[1] Hoarding is idolatry.

But where are we to draw the line between legitimate use and unlawful accumulation? Let us reverse

---

[1] It is no accident that the catalogues of vices in the Pauline Epistles associate fornication with covetousness, and designate both as idolatry.

the word of Jesus and our question is answered: "Where thy heart is, there shall thy treasure be also." Our treasure may of course be small and inconspicuous, but its size is immaterial; it all depends on the heart, on ourselves. And if we ask how we are to know where our hearts are, the answer is just as simple— everything which hinders us from loving God above all things and acts as a barrier between ourselves and our obedience to Jesus is our treasure, and the place where our heart is.

But Jesus knows that the heart of man hankers after a treasure, and so it is his will that he should have one.[1] But this treasure is to be sought in heaven, not on earth. Earthly treasures soon fade, but a treasure in heaven lasts for ever. By this treasure Jesus does not mean the one great treasure of himself, but treasures in the literal sense of the word, treasures accumulated by the disciples for themselves. What a wonderful promise we have here: as we follow Jesus, we win heavenly treasures which are incorruptible; they are waiting for us, and one day we shall enjoy them as our own. Surely these treasures can be none other than the "extraordinary," the hidden character of the Christian life, none other than the fruits of the passion of Jesus Christ which sustains the lives of his followers.

If our hearts are entirely given to God, it is clear that we *cannot* serve two masters; it is simply impossible—at any rate all the time we are following Christ. It would of course be tempting to show how far we had advanced in the Christian life by endeavouring to

---

[1] It is to be observed that Jesus does not deprive the human heart of its instinctive needs—treasure, glory and praise. But he gives it higher objects—the glory of God (John 5.44), the glorying in the cross (Gal. 6.14), and the treasure in heaven.

serve two masters and giving each his due, both God
and Mammon. Why should we not be happy children
of the world just because we are the children of God?
After all, do we not rejoice in his good gifts, and do
we not receive our treasures as a blessing from him?
No, God and the world, God and its goods are incompatible, because the world and its goods make a bid
for our hearts, and only when they have won them
do they become what they really are. That is how they
thrive, and that is why they are incompatible with
allegiance to God. Our hearts have room only for one
all-embracing devotion, and we can only cleave to
one Lord. Every competitor to that devotion must be
hated. As Jesus says, there is no alternative—either
we love God or we hate him. We are confronted by
an "either—or": either we love God, or we love earthly
goods. If we love God, we hate the world; and if we
love the world, we hate God. It makes no difference
whether that love be conscious and deliberate or not;
in fact it is morally certain that it will be neither, and
that our conscious and deliberate desire will be to serve
two masters, to love God *and* the good things of life.
We shall indignantly repudiate the suggestion that we
hate God, and will be firmly convinced that we love
him, whereas by trying to combine love for him with
love for the world, we are turning our love for him
into hatred. And then we have lost the single eye, and
our heart is no longer in fellowship with Jesus. Our
deliberate intentions make no difference to the inevitable result: Ye cannot serve two masters, if ye be
followers of Jesus Christ.

Therefore I say unto you, Be not anxious for your life,
what ye shall eat, or what ye shall drink; nor yet for your
body, what ye shall put on. Is not the life more than the

food, and the body than the raiment? Behold the birds of the heaven, that they sow not, neither do they reap, nor gather into barns; and your heavenly Father feedeth them. Are not ye of much more value than they? And which of you by being anxious can add one cubit unto his stature? And why are ye anxious concerning raiment? Consider the lilies of the field, how they grow; they toil not, neither do they spin: yet I say unto you, that even Solomon in all his glory was not arrayed like one of these. But if God doth so clothe the grass of the field, which to-day is, and to- morrow is cast into the oven, shall he not much more clothe you, O ye of little faith? Be not therefore anxious, saying, What shall we eat? or, What shall we drink? or Where- withal shall we be clothed? For after all these things do the Gentiles seek; for your heavenly Father knoweth that ye have need of all these things. But seek ye first his king- dom, and his righteousness; and all these things shall be added unto you. Be not therefore anxious for the morrow: for the morrow will be anxious for itself. Sufficient unto the day is the evil thereof. (Matt. 6.25-34)

Be not anxious! Earthly possessions dazzle our eyes and delude us into thinking that they can provide security and freedom from anxiety. Yet all the time they are the very source of all anxiety. If our hearts are set on them, our reward is an anxiety whose burden is intolerable. Anxiety creates its own treasures and they in turn beget further care. When we seek for security in possessions we are trying to drive out care with care, and the net result is the precise opposite of our anticipations. The fetters which bind us to our possessions prove to be cares themselves.

The way to misuse our possessions is to use them as an insurance against the morrow. Anxiety is always directed to the morrow, whereas goods are in the strictest sense meant to be used only for to-day. By trying to ensure for the next day we are only creating uncertainty to-day. Sufficient unto the day is the evil thereof. The only way to win assurance is by leaving to-morrow entirely in the hands of God and by receiving from him all we need for to-day. If instead of receiving God's gifts for to-day we worry about to-morrow, we find ourselves helpless victims of infinite anxiety. "Be not anxious for the morrow": either that is cruel mockery for the poor and wretched, the very people Jesus is talking to who, humanly speaking, really will starve if they do not make provision to-day. Either it is an intolerable law, which men will reject with indignation; or it is the unique proclamation of the gospel of the glorious liberty of the children of God, who have a Father in heaven, a Father who has given his beloved Son. How shall not God with him also freely give us all things?

"Be not anxious for the morrow." This is not to be taken as a philosophy of life or a moral law: it is the gospel of Jesus Christ, and only so can it be understood. Only those who follow him and know him can receive this word as a promise of the love of his Father and as a deliverance from the thraldom of material things. It is not care that frees the disciples from care, but their faith in Jesus Christ. Only they know that we *cannot* be anxious (verse 27). The coming day, even the coming hour, are placed beyond our control. It is senseless to pretend that we can make provision because we cannot alter the circumstances of this world. Only God can take care, for it is he who rules the world. Since we *cannot* take care, since we are so completely powerless, we *ought* not to do it either. If we do, we are dethroning God and presuming to rule the world ourselves.

But the Christian also knows that he not only cannot and dare not be anxious, but that there is also no
need for him to be so. Neither anxiety nor work can
secure his daily bread, for bread is the gift of the
Father. The birds and lilies neither toil nor spin, yet
both are fed and clothed and receive their daily portion without being anxious for them. They need earthly
goods only for their daily sustenance, and they do not
lay up a store for the future. This is the way they
glorify their Creator, not by their industry, toil or
care, but by a daily unquestioning acceptance of his
gifts. Birds and lilies then are an example for the
followers of Christ. "Man-in-revolt" imagines that there
is a relation of cause and effect between work and
sustenance, but Jesus explodes that illusion. According to him, bread is not to be valued as the reward for
work; he speaks instead of the carefree simplicity of
the man who walks with him and accepts everything
as it comes from God.

"Now mark ye, no beast worketh for his sustenance,
but each hath his proper function, according to which
he seeketh and findeth his own food. The bird doth
fly and sing, she maketh nests and beareth young.
That is her work, but yet she doth not nourish herself
thereby. Oxen plough, horses draw carts and fight,
sheep give wool, milk, and cheese, for it is their function so to do. But they do not nurture themselves
thereby. Nay, the earth bringeth forth grass, and
nurtureth them through God's blessing. Likewise it is
man's bounden duty to work and do things, and yet
withal to know that it is Another who nurtureth him:
it is not his own work, but the bounteous blessing of
God. It is true that the bird doth neither sow nor reap,
yet would she die of hunger if she flew not in search
of food. But that she findeth the same is not her work,

but the goodness of God. For who put the food there, that she might find it? For where God hath put nought, none findeth, even though the whole world were to work itself to death in search thereof" (Luther). But if the Creator thus sustains the birds and lilies, should he not much more as a Father nourish his own children, who daily pray to him? Should he not be able to grant them the necessities of life, when all earthly goods belong to him, and when he can distribute them according to his pleasure?

> God the Father grant to me
> All my daily needs.
> Why should I not unto him flee,
> When all the birds he feeds?
> (CLAUDIUS)

Anxiety is characteristic of the Gentiles, for they rely on their own strength and work instead of relying on God. They do not know that the Father knows that we have need of all these things, and so they try to do for themselves what they do not expect from God. But the disciples know that the rule is "Seek ye first the kingdom of God and his righteousness, and all these things shall be added unto you." Anxiety for food and clothing is clearly not the same thing as anxiety for the kingdom of God, however much we should like to persuade ourselves that when we are working for our families and concerning ourselves with bread and houses we are thereby building the kingdom, as though the kingdom could be realized only through our worldly cares. The kingdom of God and his righteousness are sharply distinguished from the gifts of the world which come our way. That kingdom is none other than the righteousness of Matt. 5 and 6, the righteousness of the cross and of following Christ beneath that cross. Fellowship with Jesus and obedience to his commandment come first, and all else follows. Worldly cares are not a part of our discipleship, but distinct and subordinate concerns. Before we start taking thought for our life, our food and clothing, our work and families, we must seek the righteousness of Christ. This is no more than an ultimate summing up of all that has been said before. Again we have here either a crushing burden, which holds out no hope for the poor and wretched, or else it is the quintessence of the gospel, which brings the promise of freedom and perfect joy. Jesus does not tell us what we ought to do but cannot; he tells us what God has given us and promises still to give. If Christ has been given us, if we are called to his discipleship we are given all things, literally *all* things. He will see to it that they are added unto us. If we follow Jesus and look only to his righteousness, we are in his hands and under the protection of him and his Father. And if we are in communion with the Father, nought can harm us. We shall always be assured that he can feed his children and will not suffer them to hunger. God will help us in the hour of need, and he knows our needs.

After he has been following Christ for a long time, the disciple of Jesus will be asked "Lacked ye anything?" and he will answer "Nothing, Lord." How could he when he knows that despite hunger and nakedness, persecution and danger, the Lord is always at his side?

13

The Disciple and Unbelievers

Judge not, that ye be not judged. For with what judgement ye judge, ye shall be judged: and with what measure ye mete, it shall be measured unto you. And why beholdest thou the mote that is in thy brother's eye, but considerest not the beam that is in thine own eye? Or how wilt thou say to thy brother, Let me cast out the mote out of thine eye; and lo, the beam is in thine own eye? Thou hypocrite, cast out first the beam out of thine own eye; and then shalt thou see clearly to cast out the mote out of thy brother's eye.

Give not that which is holy unto the dogs, neither cast your pearls before the swine, lest haply they trample them under their feet, and turn and rend you.

Ask, and it shall be given you; seek, and ye shall find; knock, and it shall be opened unto you: for every one that asketh receiveth; and he that seeketh findeth; and to him that knocketh it shall be opened. Or what man is there of you, who, if his son shall ask him for a loaf, will give him a stone; or if he shall ask for a fish, will give him a serpent? If ye then, being evil, know how to give good gifts unto your children, how much more shall your Father which is in heaven give good things to them that ask him? All things therefore whatsoever ye would that men should do unto you, even so do ye also unto them: for this is the law and the prophets. (Matt. 7.1-12)

THERE IS a continuous thread running through chapters 5 and 6; it passes through these

verses, and on to the grand finale of the Sermon on
the Mount. Chapter 5 dealt with the extraordinary
quality of the Christian life, περισσόν, and chapter 6
with the hidden single-hearted righteousness of the
disciples (ἁπλοῦς). In both its aspects, discipleship
betokened the separation of the disciples from all their
old ties, and an exclusive adherence to Jesus Christ.
The frontier between the old life and the new was
clearly drawn. But this raises the question of the relation between the Christians and their non-Christian
neighbours. Does their separation from the rest of
society confer on them special rights and privileges?
Do Christians enjoy power, gifts and standards of
judgement which qualify them to exert a peculiar
authority over others? How easy it would have been
for the disciples to adopt a superior attitude, to pass
unqualified condemnation on the rest of the world,
and to persuade themselves that this was the will of
God! That is why Jesus has to make it clear beyond all
doubt that such misunderstandings would seriously
imperil their discipleship. The disciples are not to
judge. If they do so, they will themselves be judged
by God. The sword wherewith they judge their
brethren will fall upon their own heads. Instead of
cutting themselves off from their brother as the just
from the unjust, they find themselves cut off from
Jesus.

Why should this be so? The source of the disciple's
life lies exclusively in his fellowship with Jesus Christ.
He possesses his righteousness only within that asso-
ciation, never outside it. That is why his righteousness
can never become an objective criterion to be applied
at will. He is a disciple not because he possesses such
a new standard, but only because of Jesus Christ, the
Mediator and very Son of God. That is to say, his

righteousness is hidden from himself in fellowship with Jesus. He cannot, as he could once, be a detached observer of himself and judge himself, for he can only see Jesus, and be seen by him, judged by him, and reprieved by him. It is not an approved standard of righteous living that separates a follower of Christ from the unbeliever, but it is Christ who stands between them. Christians always see other men as brethren to whom Christ comes; they meet them only by going to them with Jesus. Disciple and non-disciple can never encounter each other as free men, directly exchanging their views and judging one another by objective criteria. No, the disciple can meet the non-disciple only as a man to whom Jesus comes. Here alone Christ's fight for the soul of the unbeliever, his call, his love, his grace and his judgement comes into its own. Discipleship does not afford us a point of vantage from which to attack others; we come to them with an unconditional offer of fellowship, with the single-mindedness of the love of Jesus.

When we judge other people we confront them in a spirit of detachment, observing and reflecting as it were from the outside. But love has neither time nor opportunity for this. If we love, we can never observe the other person with detachment, for he is always and at every moment a living claim to our love and service. But does not the evil in the other person make me condemn him just for his own good, for the sake of love? Here we see the depth of the dividing line. Any misguided love for the sinner is ominously close to the love of sin. But the love of Christ for the sinner in itself is the condemnation of sin, is his expression of extreme hatred of sin. The disciples of Christ are to love unconditionally. Thus they may effect what their own divided and judiciously and conditionally offered love never could achieve, namely the radical condemnation of sin.

If the disciples make judgements of their own, they set up standards of good and evil. But Jesus Christ is not a standard which I can apply to others. He is judge of myself, revealing my own virtues to me as something altogether evil. Thus I am not permitted to apply to the other person what does not apply to me. For, with my judgement according to good and evil, I only affirm the other person's evil, for he does exactly the same. But he does not know of the hidden iniquity of the good but seeks his justification in it. If I condemn his evil actions I thereby confirm him in his apparently good actions which are yet never the good commended by Christ. Thus we remove him from the judgement of Christ and subject him to human judgement. But I bring God's judgement upon my head, for I then do not live any more on and out of the grace of Jesus Christ, but out of my knowledge of good and evil which I hold on to. To everyone God is the kind of God he believes in.

Judgement is the forbidden objectivization of the other person which destroys single-minded love. I am not forbidden to have my own thoughts about the other person, to realize his shortcomings, but only to the extent that it offers to me an occasion for forgiveness and unconditional love, as Jesus proves to me. If I withhold my judgement I am not indulging in *tout comprendre c'est tout pardonner* and confirm the other person in his bad ways. Neither I am right nor the other person, but God is always right and shall proclaim both his grace and his judgement.

Judging others makes us blind, whereas love is illuminating. By judging others we blind ourselves to our own evil and to the grace which others are just as entitled to as we are. But in the love of Christ we know all about every conceivable sin and guilt; for we know how Jesus suffered, and how all men have been forgiven at the foot of the cross. Christian love sees the fellow-man under the cross and therefore sees with clarity. If when we judged others, our real motive was to destroy evil, we should look for evil where it is certain to be found, and that is in our own hearts. But if we are on the look-out for evil in others, our real motive is obviously to justify ourselves, for we are seeking to escape punishment for our own sins by passing judgement on others, and are assuming by implication that the Word of God applies to ourselves in one way, and to others in another. All this is highly dangerous and misleading. We are trying to claim for ourselves a special privilege which we deny to others. But Christ's disciples have no rights of their own or standards of right and wrong which they could enforce with other people; they have received nothing but Christ's fellowship. Therefore the disciple is not to sit in judgement over his fellow-man because he would wrongly usurp the jurisdiction.

But the Christian is not only forbidden to *judge* other men: even the word of salvation has its limits. He has neither power nor right to force it on other men in season and out of season. Every attempt to impose the gospel by force, to run after people and proselytize them, to use our own resources to arrange the salvation of other people, is both futile and dangerous. It is futile, because the swine do not recognize the pearls that are cast before them, and dangerous, because it profanes the word of forgiveness, by causing those we fain would serve to sin against that which is holy. Worse still, we shall only meet with the blind rage of hardened and darkened hearts, and that will be useless and harmful. Our easy trafficking with the word of cheap grace simply bores the world to disgust, so that in the end it turns against those who try to force on it what it does not want. Thus a strict limit is placed upon the activities of the disciples, just as in Matt. 10 they are told to shake the dust off their feet where the word of peace is refused a hearing. Their restless energy which refuses to recognize any limit to their activity, the zeal which refuses to take note of resistance, springs from a confusion of the gospel with a victorious ideology. An ideology requires fanatics, who neither know nor notice opposition, and it is certainly a potent force. But the Word of God in its weakness takes the risk of meeting the scorn of men and being rejected. There are hearts which are hardened and doors which are closed to the Word. The Word recognizes opposition when it meets it, and is prepared to suffer it. It is a hard lesson, but a true one, that the gospel, unlike an ideology, reckons with impossibilities. The Word is weaker than any ideology, and this means that with only the gospel at their command the witnesses are weaker than the propagandists of an opinion. But although they are weak, they are ready to suffer with the Word and so are free from that morbid restlessness which is so characteristic of fanaticism.

The disciples can even yield their ground and run away, provided they do so with the Word, provided their weakness is the weakness of the Word, and provided they do not leave the Word in the lurch in their flight. They are simply the servants and instruments of the Word; they have no wish to be strong where the Word chooses to be weak. To try and force the Word on the world by hook or by crook is to make the living Word of God into a mere idea, and the world

would be perfectly justified in refusing to listen to an
idea for which it had no use. But at other times, the
disciples must stick to their guns and refuse to run
away, though of course only when the Word so wills.
If they do not realize this weakness of the Word, they
have failed to perceive the mystery of the divine
humility. The same weak Word which is content to
endure the gainsaying of sinners is also the mighty
Word of mercy which can convert the hearts of sinners. Its strength is veiled in weakness; if it came in
power that would mean that the day of judgement had
arrived. The great task of the disciples is to recognize
the limits of their commission. But if they use the
Word amiss it will certainly turn against them.

What are the disciples to do when they encounter
opposition and cannot penetrate the hearts of men?
They must admit that in no circumstances do they
possess any rights or powers over others, and that they
have no direct access to them. The only way to reach
others is through him in whose hands they are themselves like all other men. We shall hear more about
this as we proceed. The disciples are taught to pray,
and so they learn that the only way to reach others is
by praying to God. Judgement and forgiveness are
always in the hands of God. He closes and he opens.
But the disciples must ask, they must seek and knock,
and then God will hear them. They have to learn that
their anxiety and concern for others must drive them
to intercession. The promise Christ gives to their
prayer is the doughtiest weapon in their armoury.

The difference between the disciples' seeking and the
Gentiles' quest for God is that the disciples know what
they are looking for. We can only seek God when we
know him already. How can you look for something
or find it if you do not know what you are looking for?

The disciples seek a God whom they have found in the promise they have received from Jesus.

To sum up: it is clear from the foregoing that the disciple has no special privilege or power of his own in all his intercourse with others. The mainspring of his life and work is the strength which comes from fellowship with Jesus Christ. Jesus offers his disciples a simple rule of thumb which will enable even the least sophisticated of them to tell whether his intercourse with others is on the right lines or not. All he need do is to say "I" instead of "Thou," and put himself in the other man's place. "All things whatsoever ye would that men should do unto you, even so do ye also unto them: for this is the law and the prophets." The moment he does that, the disciple forfeits all advantage over other men, and can no longer excuse in himself what he condemns in others. He is as strict in condemning evil in himself as he was before with others, and as lenient with the evil in others as he was before to himself. The evil in the other person is exactly the same evil as in ourselves. There is only *one* judgement, *one* law, and *one* grace. Henceforth the disciple will look upon other men as forgiven sinners who owe their lives to the love of God. "This is the law and the prophets"—for this is none other than the supreme commandment: to love God above all things and our neighbours as ourselves.

14
The Great Divide

Enter ye in by the narrow gate: for wide is the gate, and broad is the way, that leadeth to destruction, and many be they that enter in thereby. For narrow is the gate, and straitened the way, that leadeth unto life, and few be they that find it.

Beware of false prophets, which come to you in sheep's clothing, but inwardly are ravening wolves. By their fruits ye shall know them. Do men gather grapes of thorns, or figs of thistles? Even so every good tree bringeth forth good fruit; but the corrupt tree bringeth forth evil fruit. A good tree cannot bring forth evil fruit, neither can a corrupt tree bring forth good fruit. Every tree that bringeth not forth good fruit is hewn down, and cast into the fire. Therefore by their fruits ye shall know them. Not everyone that saith unto me, Lord, Lord, shall enter into the kingdom of heaven; but he that doeth the will of my Father which is in heaven. Many will say to me in that day, Lord, Lord, did we not prophesy by thy name, and by thy name cast out devils, and by thy name do many mighty works? And then will I profess unto them, I never knew you: depart from me, ye that work iniquity. (Matt. 7.13-23)

THE CHURCH of Jesus cannot arbitrarily break off all contact with those who refuse his call. It is called to follow the Lord by promise and commandment. That must suffice. All judgement of others and separation from them must be left to him who chose the Church according to his good purpose, and not for any merit or achievement of its own. The separation of Church and world is not effected by the Church itself, but by the word of its calling.

A little band of men, the followers of Christ, are separated from the rest of the world. The disciples are few in number, and will always be few. This saying of Jesus forestalls all exaggerated hopes of success. Never let a disciple of Jesus pin his hopes on large numbers. "Few there be. . . ." The rest of the world are many, and will always be many. But they are on the road to perdition. The only comfort the disciples have in face of this prospect is the promise of life and eternal fellowship with Jesus.

The path of discipleship is narrow, and it is fatally easy to miss one's way and stray from the path, even after years of discipleship. And it is hard to find. On either side of the narrow path deep chasms yawn. To be called to a life of extraordinary quality, to live up to it, and yet to be unconscious of it is indeed a narrow way. To confess and testify to the truth as it is in Jesus, and at the same time to love the enemies of that truth, his enemies and ours, and to love them with the infinite love of Jesus Christ, is indeed a narrow way. To believe the promise of Jesus that his followers shall possess the earth, and at the same time to face our enemies unarmed and defenceless, preferring to incur injustice rather than to do wrong ourselves, is indeed a narrow way. To see the weakness and wrong in others, and at the same time refrain from judging them; to deliver the gospel message without casting pearls before swine, is indeed a narrow way. The way is unutterably hard, and at every moment we are in danger of straying from it. If we regard this way as one we follow in obedience to an external command, if we are afraid of ourselves all the time, it is indeed an impossible way. But if we behold Jesus Christ going on before step by step, we shall not go astray. But if we worry about the dangers that beset us, if we gaze at the road instead of at him who goes before, we are already straying from the path. For he is himself the way, the narrow way and the strait gate. He, and he alone, is our journey's end. When we know that, we are able to proceed along the narrow way through the strait gate of the cross, and on to eternal life, and the very narrowness of the road will increase our certainty. The way which the Son of God trod on earth, and the way which we too must tread as citizens of two worlds on the razor edge between this world and the kingdom of heaven, could hardly be a broad way. The narrow way is bound to be right.

Verses 15-20. The separation of Church and world is now complete. But the word of Jesus forces its way into the Church herself, bringing judgement and decision. The separation is never permanently assured: it must constantly be renewed. The disciples of Jesus must not fondly imagine that they can simply run away from the world and huddle together in a little band. False prophets will rise up among them, and amid the ensuing confusion they will feel more isolated than ever. There is someone standing by my side, who looks just like a member of the Church. He is a prophet and a preacher. He looks like a Christian, he talks and acts like one. But dark powers are mysteriously at work; it was these who sent him into our midst. Inwardly he is a ravening wolf: his words are lies and his works are full of deceit. He knows only too well how to keep his secret dark, and go ahead with his work. It is not faith in Jesus Christ which made him one of us, but the devil. Maybe he hopes his intellectual

ability or his success as a prophet will bring him
power and influence, money and fame. His ambitions
are set on the world, not on Jesus Christ. Knowing
that Christians are credulous people, he conceals his
dark purpose beneath the cloak of Christian piety,
hoping that his innocuous disguise will avert detection.
He knows that Christians are forbidden to judge, and
he will remind them of it at the appropriate time.
After all, other men's hearts are always a closed book.
Thus he succeeds in seducing many from the right
way. He may even be unconscious himself of what he
is doing. The devil can give him every encouragement and at the same time keep him in the dark about
his own motives.

Such a pronouncement of Christ's could cause his
disciples great anxiety. Who knows his neighbour?
Who knows whether the outward appearance of a
Christian conceals falsehood and deception under-
neath? No wonder if mistrust, suspicion and censori-
ousness crept into the Church. And no wonder if every
brother who falls into sin incurred the uncharitable
criticism of his brethren, now that Jesus has said this.
All this distrust would ruin the Church but for the
word of Jesus which assures us that the bad tree will
bring forth bad fruit. It is bound to give itself away
sooner or later. There is no need to go about prying
into the hearts of others. All we need do is to wait
until the tree bears fruit, and we shall not have to wait
long. This is not to say that we must draw a distinction
between the words of the prophet and his deeds: the
real distincton is that between appearance and reality.
Jesus tells us that men cannot keep up appearances
for long. The time of vintage is sure to come, and then
we shall be able to sift the good from the bad. Sooner
or later we shall find out where a man stands. It is no

use the tree refusing to bear any fruit, for the fruit comes of its own accord. Any day the time may come to decide for the world or for the Church. We may have to decide, not in some spectacular matter, but in quite trivial, everyday affairs. And then we shall see and discern the good from the bad. In that day the reality will stand the test, not appearances.

In such times as these, Jesus requires his disciples to distinguish between appearance and reality, between themselves and pseudo-Christians. They will then rise above all inquisitive examination of others, but they will need a sincere determination to recognize the verdict of God when it comes. At any moment the nominal Christians may be separated from the real ones. We may even find that we are nominal Christians ourselves. Here is a challenge to closer fellowship with Jesus and to a more loyal discipleship. The bad tree is cut down and cast into the fire. All its display of finery proves ultimately to be of no avail.

Verse 21. The separation which the call of Jesus creates goes deeper still. After the division between Church and world, between nominal Christians and real ones, the division now enters into the very heart of the confessional body. St Paul says: "No man can say, Jesus is Lord, but in the Holy Spirit" (I Cor. 12.3). It is impossible to surrender our lives to Jesus or call him Lord of our own free will. St Paul is deliberately reckoning with the possibility that men may call Jesus Lord without the Holy Spirit, that is, without having received the call. It was harder to understand this in days when it brought no earthly gain to be a Christian and when Christianity was a dangerous profession. "Not every one that saith unto me, Lord, Lord, shall enter the kingdom of heaven. . . ." "Lord, Lord" is the Church's confession of faith.

But not everyone who makes this confession will enter the kingdom of heaven. The dividing line will run right through the confessing Church. Even if we make the confession of faith, it gives us no title to any special claim upon Jesus. We can never appeal to our confession or be saved simply on the ground that we have made it. Neither is the fact that we are members of a Church which has a right confession a claim to God's favour. To think thus is to fall into the sin of Israel, which thought the grace of God's call gave it a special privilege in his sight. That would be a sin against God's gracious call. God will not ask us in that day whether we were good Protestants, but whether we have done his will. We shall be asked the same question as everybody else. The Church is marked off from the world not by a special privilege, but by the gracious election and calling of God. Πᾶς ὁ λέγων and ἀλλ᾽ ὁ ποιῶν, "say" and "do"—this does not mean the ordinary contrast between word and deed, but two different relations between man and God. Ὁ λέγων κύριε –the man who says "Lord, Lord"—means the man who puts forward a claim on the ground that he has said "it," ὁ ποιῶν—the doer—is the man of humble obedience. The first is the one who justifies himself through his confession, and the second, the doer, the obedient man who builds his life on the grace of God. Here a man's speaking denotes self-righteousness, his doing is a token of grace, to which there can be no other response save that of humble and obedient service. The man who says "Lord, Lord" has either called himself to Jesus without the Holy Spirit, or else he has made out of the call of Jesus a personal privilege. But our doer of the will of God is called and endued with grace, he obeys and follows. He understands his call not as his right, but as an act of

God's judgement and grace, as the will of God, which alone he must obey. The grace of Jesus is a demand upon the doer, and so his doing becomes the true humility, the right faith, and the right confession of the grace of the God who calls.

Verse 22. Confessor and doer are separated from one another. And now the division is carried to its furthest extent. Only those are now speaking who have survived the test so far. They are numbered among the doers, but they appeal not to their confession, but to the deeds they have done. They have performed deeds in the name of Jesus. Thy know that confession does not justify, and so they have gone and made the name of Jesus great among the people by their deeds. Now they appear before Jesus and tell him what they have done.

At this point Jesus reveals to his disciples the possibility of a demonic faith which produces wonderful works quite indistinguishable from the works of the true disciples, works of charity, miracles, perhaps even of personal sanctification, but which is nevertheless a denial of Jesus and of the life of discipleship. This is just what St Paul means in I Cor. 13, when he says that it is possible to preach, to prophesy, to have all knowledge, and even faith so as to remove mountains, and all this without love, that is to say, without Christ, without the Holy Spirit. More than this, St Paul must even reckon with the possibility that the very works of Christian charity, giving away one's goods, and even martyrdom, may be done without love, without Christ, without the Holy Spirit. Without love: that is to say, in all this activity the activity of discipleship is absent, namely that activity the doer of which is in the last resort none other than Jesus Christ himself. Here is the most serious, most incredible satanic possibility in the

Church, the final division, which only occurs at the last day. But Christ's followers must ask by what ultimate criterion Jesus will accept or reject them. Who will pass the test, and who will not? The answer lies in the words of Jesus to the last of the rejected: "I have never known you." Here we are at last, here is the secret we have been waiting for since the Sermon on the Mount began. Here is the crucial question—has Jesus known us or not? First came the division between Church and world, then the division within the Church, and then the final division on the last day. There is nothing left for us to cling to, not even our confession or our obedience. There is only his word: "I have known thee," which is his eternal word and call. The end of the Sermon on the Mount echoes the beginning. The word of the last judgement is foreshadowed in the call to discipleship. But from begining to end it is always *his* word and *his* call, his alone. If we follow Christ, cling to his word, and let everything else go, it will see us through the day of judgement. His word is his grace.

15
The Conclusion

Every one therefore which heareth these words of mine, and doeth them, shall be likened unto a wise man, which built his house upon the rock: and the rain descended, and the floods came, and the winds blew, and beat upon that house; and it fell not: for it was founded upon the rock. And every one that heareth these words of mine, and doeth them not, shall be likened unto a foolish man, which built his house upon the sand: and the rain descended, and the floods came, and the winds blew, and smote upon that house; and it fell: and great was the fall thereof.

And it came to pass, when Jesus ended these words, the multitudes were astonished at his teaching: for he taught them as one having authority, and not as their scribes. (Matt. 7.24-29)

WE HAVE listened to the Sermon on the Mount and perhaps have understood it. But who has heard it aright? Jesus gives the answer at the end. He does not allow his hearers to go away and make of his sayings what they will, picking and choosing from them whatever they find helpful, and testing them to see if they work. He does not give them free rein to misuse his word with their mercenary hands, but gives it to them on condition that it retains exclusive power over them. Humanly speaking, we could understand and interpret the Sermon on the Mount in a thousand different ways. Jesus knows only one possibility: simple surrender and obedience, not interpreting it or applying it, but doing and obeying it. That is the only way to hear his word. But again he does not mean that it is to be discussed as an ideal, he really means us to get on with it.

This word, whose claim we recognize, this word which issues from his saying "I have known thee," this word which sets us at once to work and obedience, is the rock on which to build our house. The only proper response to this word which Jesus brings with him from eternity is simply to do it. Jesus has spoken: his is the word, ours the obedience. Only in the doing of it does the word of Jesus retain its honour, might and power among us. Now the storm can rage over the house, but it cannot shatter that union with him, which his word has created.

There is only one other possibility, that of failing to do it. It is impossible to want to do it and yet not do it. To deal with the word of Jesus otherwise than by doing it is to give him the lie. It is to deny the Sermon on the Mount and to say No to his word. If we start asking questions, posing problems, and offering inter-pretations, we are not doing his word. Once again the shades of the rich young man and the lawyer of Luke 10 are raising their heads. However vehe-mently we assert our faith, and our fundamental recog-nition of his word, Jesus still calls it "not-doing." But the word which we fail to do is no rock to build a house on. There can then be no union with Jesus. He has never known us. That is why as soon as the hurricane begins we lose the word, and find that we have never really believed it. The word we had was not Christ's, but a word we had wrested from him and made our own by reflecting on it instead of doing it. So our house crashes in ruins, because it is not founded on the word of Jesus Christ.

"The multitudes were astonished. . . ." What had happened? The Son of God had spoken. He had taken the judgement of the world into his own hands. And his disciples were standing at his side.